IT'S
HERE. . .
SOMEWHERE

ABOUT THE AUTHORS

Alice Fulton and Pauline Hatch are full-time homemakers, "reformed clutter shufflers" and specialists in the field of home management. Both authors have thoroughly home-tested their system (Alice and her husband have seven children, Pauline and her husband, five children). They have also taught their organizational approach to thousands of people through seminars, televison appearances, and their "Clutter Therapists" consulting firm. They live in Washington state.

Alice Fulton
and Pauline Hatch

IT'S HERE . . . SOMEWHERE

WRITER'S DIGEST BOOKS
Cincinnati, Ohio

Illustrations by Shunichi Yamamoto, Great Western Promotions.
Revised Edition contains four new illustrations by Suzanne Whitaker (pages 37, 41, 74, and bicycle rack on 143).

Other fine Writer's Digest Books are available from your local bookstore or direct from the publisher.

00 99 98 97 96   8 7 6 5 4

Library of Congress Cataloging-in-Publication Data

Fulton, Alice
   It's here—somewhere / by Alice Fulton and Pauline Hatch.
     p.   cm.
   Includes biographical references (p.) and index.
   ISBN 0-89879-447-1 (pbk.)
   1. Home economics. 2. Dwellings. I. Hatch, Pauline. II. Title.
TX303.F85 1991
640—dc20

90-13084
CIP

Edited by Beth Franks
Designed by Sandy Conopeotis

DEDICATION

I n 1985 we dedicated the first edition of this book to ourselves rather than husbands and kids (as is the typical dedication format), because at the time, husbands and kids weren't particularly interested or supportive of what we were trying to accomplish. Once again we dedicate this book primarily to ourselves.

However, attitudes and behaviors have changed. Husbands Ferris Hatch and Gordon Fulton have since tuned into our determination and now give emotional support and physical help in dealing with the daily nitty-gritty of managing homes and families. Their assistance has freed us to more intensely pursue our careers, thus we offer them a public THANK YOU and a share in this dedication page.

Our kids, Sheree, Holly, Reed, Don, and Kevin Hatch; and Andrew, Sarah, Philip, Joseph, Paul, Anna, and Mary Fulton are still slow to give whole-hearted physical help around home. (Although we've come to understand this is a normal, on-going battle, it still drives us nuts.) However, they now believe in what we're trying to do and our abilities to do it. Thus, for this emotional support we offer them, too, a public THANK YOU and a share in this dedication page.

In short, all the world ought to know that we appreciate any family support we've gotten. While we would've pursued this project anyway, it sure was a lot easier when everyone cooperated.

TABLE OF CONTENTS

Preface

Acknowledgments

INTRODUCTION
1

One — **FROM SHUFFLING TO SHOVELING** — *4*

The lasting benefits of streamlined order for you and your home —
from easier maintenance to greater efficiency to dollar savings.

Two — **BASIC TRAINING** — *12*

Steps you can take and laws to live by
to achieve continual order and control.

Three — **ON YOUR MARK, GET SET . . .** — *27*

Mental preparation that will get your household
transformation off and running.

Four — **MASTERING THE MASTER BEDROOM** — *34*

Here's how to bring order and simplicity to your bedroom
and make it an even more restful place.

Five — **BRAVING THE BATH** — *46*

How to make the bathroom pretty, efficient and easy to clean —
and keep it that way.

Six — **CRIB NOTES** — *55*

Starting off with a streamlined baby's room can mean order, control
and good habits now, and as baby grows.

Seven — **CREATING A KID-READY ROOM** — *60*

Maintaining order in kids' rooms — where order never seems possible.

Eight — **FROM "NO-PLACE" TO "SHOW-PLACE"** — *70*

The living room is the world's window on you — here's how to spiff up the view.

Nine — **ALL IN THE FAMILY** — *85*

Make it easier to make yourself at home in the one room you
really live in: the family room.

Ten – **MAKING YOUR KITCHEN MEASURE UP** – *90*
Creating centers for people and activities to keep
your household transformation cooking.

Eleven – **CABINETS, CLOSETS, AND CUPBOARDS** – *119*
It's here . . . somewhere: here's how to streamline the "somewhere."

Twelve – **MY SOAP OPERA** – *127*
How to solve the case of the missing sock –
and other laundry area trials and tragedies.

Thirteen – **NO MORE SO-SO SEWING AREA** – *132*
Create a sewing haven by eliminating those so-so notions,
patterns, fabrics and more.

Fourteen – **NO MORE NO-CAR GARAGE** – *137*
How to open up parking spaces for more than just your junk.

Fifteen – **THE SUPER STORAGE AREA** – *151*
Keeping crawl spaces, basements and other spots for
"temporarily inactive" keepsakes manageable and convenient.

Conclusion – **IT REALLY *IS* HERE . . . SOMEWHERE!** – *159*
The end of our instruction, but the beginning of a more orderly life-style.

BACK-OF-THE-BOOK-BONUSES
161

SUGGESTED READING:
More books to help you.
169

INDEX
171

PREFACE

I t's here . . . somewhere, is what most of you probably say at least once a day when you can't find something. Certainly the two of us were saying it often at the end of all too many unsuccessful searches. Not that our homes were dirty, or that we were lazy—we put in long hours cleaning and organizing our homes. Yet locating our families' assorted possessions was like trying to find the proverbial needle in the haystack.

We suspect that you're trying at least as hard as we did, yet you're still suffering from some degree of household clutter. Like us, you've probably read, heard, and tried to follow lots of home management advice, some helpful, some not. After twenty years of at-home experience and six years of giving our professional "Clutter Therapy" to thousands of "patients" across America, we know we offer sound and timely solutions. We know that when you implement these solutions, they will save you two months a year, add energy to your life, cure the diseases of chronic time-crunch and terminal stressitis, eliminate ugly clutter, and solve your lack-of-space problems. In short, when you forget the organizing, and streamline instead, your home will be easier to manage and more enjoyable to live in. That's what this book is about. We think you'll find it gives you renewed "home managing hope" and is "just what the doctor ordered" for taking control of your time, your things, and your spaces.

ACKNOWLEDGMENTS

Special thanks to:

DON ASLETT for sharing his time, talents, and practical counsel with us.

BUDGE WALLIS for listening to us over lunch way back when, and for his gracious hand delivery of our first, original manuscript to Writer's Digest Books.

HOWARD I. WELLS III, our original editorial director, for his wisdom and patience.

WILLA SPEISER, for her professional insight as our original editor, who helped us turn our thoughts and ideas into clear, concise concepts.

BETH FRANKS, for professional insight as our new editor and "word-master" partner in streamlining the world!

INTRODUCTION

Every home has someone's belongings in it, and belongings have a nasty way of proliferating: The more space you have, the more things you acquire to fill that space. We've all had the experience of going to put something "away" only to find "away" is already full. It also seems, according to our research, that every home has a "pilot"—he'll "pile it" here, he'll "pile it" there, he'll "pile it" anywhere there's a vacant space. And so, over time, your home, however spacious it may once have seemed, becomes crowded, disorganized, and not nearly as welcoming as it once was.

In fact, space is at a premium for more and more of us these days. There's less of it to go around, and what's there gets more expensive by the day. The cost of new housing is constantly on the rise, and the cost of heating and maintaining older homes is increasing, too. Most people can't afford much, if any, "extra" room—and certainly can't afford to waste space.

Besides the space-crunch, we're confronting a time- and energy-crunch as well. With nine out of ten women working outside the home, more men taking on second jobs, and greater numbers of people starting home-based businesses today, there's a desperate need for easy maintenance environments. We hear the same complaints from women coast to coast: They're frustrated because they lack control over their physical spaces; they're tired from overwork; and they don't have enough time for anything extra, let alone senseless maintenance of clutter.

Space-, time-, and energy-crunches notwithstanding, we're by no means suggesting that you divest yourself of your belongings—not the ones that matter, anyway. What we do suggest is that you streamline first, then organize your entire home. In other words, forget that cure-all advice to have "a place for everything and everything in its place." That was fine for pioneer days or the years of the Great Depression, when folks didn't have much, but in today's possession-oriented world, there's no way you could have a place for *every*-thing—there just aren't that many places. Thus the advice for this day and age is to "have a place for every *keeper*, and put every *keeper* in its place." (Keepers are possessions you like, use, need, want, or have room for—they are what make your home *yours*. But combined with *tossers*—another word for clutter—they equal overload.)

Before we go on, let's define clutter. Clutter is the fish food sitting on the kitchen windowsill for the fish that have been dead for three months. Clutter is the stack of *Better Homes and Gardens* magazines, standing in the corner of some room (often the den, or even the master bedroom), that you intend to go through someday, to cut out all the "good stuff." Clutter is all the "who-in-the-heck-is-this-a-picture-of?" photos sliding around on the bottom of the middle desk drawer. Clutter is anything you don't like, use, need, want, or have room for. Clutter is a space-waster, a time-eater, a morale-sapper, and an energy-drainer. Clutter is, indeed, all the things in your home that don't matter.

We suggest you bring a "quality over quantity" attitude to your home management style. Always ask yourself, "Am I doing the household shuffle, when I should be using the household shovel on all this junk and overload?" because it's not enough to shuffle things around from this shelf to that drawer. Getting rid of the clutter—the things that don't matter—is what makes the difference.

You see, before we streamlined our homes, we were living in chaos and confusion—we were masters of the shuffle lifestyle. Pauline always had to move the newly folded laundry off the bed each night before she and her husband, Ferris, could turn in. Alice was constantly buying duplicates of scissors, cellophane tape, ballpoint pens, toothbrushes, ponytail holders, glue, hammers, weed diggers, socks, and on and on, because she and her family could never find the ones they already had—those were all "here somewhere," which meant "forget it, they're buried." Pauline recalls how it typically took at least two weeks of intensive cleaning and "organizing" to get her home ready to have guests for two days. (And then, she *still* had to route her company past rooms, closets, cupboards, or drawers that she didn't want anyone to see.) We both remember the drudgery of our laundry routines—doing loads by the ton that were composed not only of dirty clothes, but of "nonkeeper" clothes and "never-wear" clothes. (More on this in the master bedroom, kids' room, and laundry area chapters.) When we recall how we used to live, it gives us the heebie-jeebies.

In spite of the chaos and frustration, we still had hope that there was an answer somewhere. We would read every book on household organization we could find, attend every seminar on the subject, and take every home management or organization class that came our way. But we consistently found, to our deep disappointment, that the ideas and systems we came away with and implemented had only short-term impact (maybe two weeks at the most). Then we were back in the same old ruts.

Finally convinced that organization alone wasn't getting us anywhere, we devised our own system—STREAMLINING, which involved getting rid of and not just organizing stuff. We first put it to work in our master bedrooms (after all, this is where we began each day, so this seemed a logical starting point). After living with streamlined and not just organized master bedrooms for three weeks, we had what we call an "Ah-ha Experience" (an "I-see-the-light experience"). "Ah-ha," we said, "we're on to something. These rooms *still* look gorgeous. We're *still* in control of the stuff and spaces, and it took *minimal* time and energy to keep it this way." Getting rid of the clutter is what made the difference. We're convinced you'll share this "Ah-ha Experience" when you trade shuffling for shoveling.

HOW DO YOU START?

The key to our not-so-mysterious technique of space control is to evaluate and assess everything you own and every space in your home. Do these things deserve to share your living space, and are your spaces being used to their best advantage?

This evaluation/assessment process will create two groups of things: keepers and tossers. In our experience, when a typical home of nine to ten rooms is completely streamlined, forty-five to fifty full, thirty-gallon-sized trash bags of tossers are hauled away. Of these forty-five bags (it averages four and a half per room), 70 percent go to charity, and 30 percent go into the trash.

You can see how much space this elimination-by-evaluation process frees up. When you combine the final products—keepers and empty spaces—good organization will follow almost automatically. The catch to this claim is creating the empty spaces. It's been our experience that 97 percent of people can organize just about anything, if they have the space for it. Thus we say that organization is a result of our system, and not one of the tools.

We've found a room-by-room approach to streamlining is the only way to go. Not everyone has the same kinds or number of rooms, but we all know that kitchens, baths, bedrooms, family rooms, and those infamous storage areas all offer their own special kinds of clutter and potential space control needs.

To help you conquer your clutter as efficiently and painlessly as possible, we've organized this book by room and area. That way, if there's a room you *don't* have a problem with, you simply skip the chapter that deals with it. Better still, thinking about the job one room at a time makes the overall task seem much less overwhelming and, much more do-able. So press on, and "May your household shovel always be full!"

ONE

FROM SHUFFLING TO SHOVELING

The lasting benefits of streamlined order in the home

As professional consultants – the "Clutter Therapists" – we've helped thousands of home managers streamline their homes. The feedback has been overwhelming: In every case, what they needed to do was unload the overload, not employ any particular revolutionary organization techniques.

That's because once you've eliminated the clutter, just about any organizing system will work, whether it's based on which family member owns what, what activities items are used for, or even what letter of the alphabet an item's name begins with. Organization is the result of streamlining, not a tool.

Thus, you won't find lots of clever organization tips in this book – we've left this to the other two million writers. We teach streamlining, unloading the overload, eliminating the clutter. We've found that the reason you and millions of readers like you haven't achieved permanent order and control of your interior spaces is that you've been trying to organize too much stuff – you've been doing the household shuffle when you should've been using the household shovel. We believe in clear surfaces rather than "organized" surfaces. We say get rid of everything you don't like, use, need, want, or have room for. What's left will be quality keepers and lots of empty spaces. Put the two together and you have your own brand of lasting organization.

The system we're about to teach you *is* a lot of work, at least initially. But if you keep up the system and adopt streamlining as your home management method, you'll never have to go through this intensive unloading again. And yes, trading shuffling for shoveling will make a tremendous difference in your home and in your life. In the rest of this chapter, we'll look at just some of the lasting benefits, including the following:

- More time and energy
- More space
- No more clutter
- Easier maintenance
- More efficient layout

- A better-looking home
- Peace of mind
- Less stress

MORE TIME AND ENERGY

In the April 1989 issue of *Good Housekeeping* magazine, we discovered this information: In a yearlong study combining phone surveys, existing research, and actual stopwatch timings taken in various situations, the Priority Management Co. of Pittsburgh, Pennsylvania determined that the average person spends four years cleaning house, three years preparing meals, and one year searching for misplaced things. We suspect that this average person was most likely cleaning an overloaded house, preparing meals in an overloaded kitchen, and searching for misplaced things in overloaded closets, cupboards, and drawers. Overload does waste time—and time is your life.

Scrubbing, vacuuming, dusting, sorting, washing, putting away, finding, and shuffling in a *streamlined* home means a huge savings in time and energy. In fact, our studies indicate you'll save more than two months per year! Can you even imagine what you'd do with two extra months? How many books could you read? What hobbies might you pursue? Or what craft might you further develop? How many walks would you take? What community volunteer work would you do? How many letters would you write? What new sport would you take up? How many relatives or friends would you visit? How many concerts, operas, or museum showings would you attend? And what about your kids? Would you now have the time to help them with their homework, play with them, teach them a skill, or listen to them? Simply stated, streamlining leaves you with less to take care of, which means more time for what really matters in life—much of which you've put off *until* you have time for it. You'll also spend less time looking for all the lost what-have-yous. (No more arriving late and angry at meetings because of misplaced car keys, kids' shoes, coats, and so on.)

In preparing material for this book and for our "Get the Rats Out of Your Race!" seminars, we've kept detailed records of time spent on routine chores before and after streamlining. The results are convincing.

TASK	BEFORE	AFTER
Dusting a 2,000-sq. ft. home	35 minutes	15-17 minutes

The savings are dramatic and come about because the surfaces to be dusted were clear of clutter. There was no more need to dust the clutter or move it to dust the surface under it. The streamlining motto is "Keep it clear and you can keep it clean."

Now if 35 minutes for dusting doesn't seem like much to you, consider this: If you dust twice a week, dusting takes 70 minutes a week. Multiply this 70 minutes by the 52 weeks in a year, and you spend 3,640 minutes, or over 60 hours a year—that's 2½ days—just dusting.

TASK	BEFORE	AFTER
Vacuuming the floors and stairs in a 2,000-sq. ft. home	40 minutes	25 minutes

Again, the time is cut almost in half, thanks to not having to move or navigate around clutter.

If you vacuum three times a week, the total time comes to 120 minutes, or 2 hours per week. Multiply this 2 hours by 52 weeks, and you'll find that you spend 104 hours a year, or 4 ⅓ days a year vacuuming.

TASK	BEFORE	AFTER
Laundry for a family of four	7-9 loads a week	4-6 loads a week

Everyone owns clothing he or she never wears. And yet for one reason or another, especially if the family includes children, much of this never-wear clothing ends up in the laundry. Nine loads of wash each week, at 15 minutes for washing and 20 minutes for drying per load, takes the machines 315 minutes a week to do. Multiply this figure by 52 and you get 16,380 minutes a year, or 273 hours. That's more than 11½ days a year that your machines are put into service and subject to wear and tear. You can see that eliminating laundry loads is a practical thing to do, if only to lengthen the life of your appliances.

But what about the wear and tear on *you*? We haven't even counted the time it takes to gather, sort, and load clothes into the machines or to fold clean laundry. We've found there isn't that much difference (before and after) in the time it takes to gather clothes or load clothes into the machines, so we won't consider these two chores. But there is a HUGE savings in time and energy when it comes to sorting and folding. Whether you stagger laundry loads throughout the week or do them all on the same day doesn't matter—the numbers are the same.

TASK	BEFORE	AFTER
Sorting laundry for a family of four (7-9 loads a week)	20 minutes for 9 loads	10 minutes for 6 loads

Multiply the 20 minutes it takes to sort nine loads of wash per week by the 52 weeks in a year and you get 1,040 minutes, or 17⅓ hours per year. After streamlining all clothing and eliminating approximately three loads of laundry, sorting can be done in 10 minutes, which when multiplied by 52 equals 520 minutes, or a little over 8 hours per year—you've almost cut your sorting time in half.

TASK	BEFORE	AFTER
Folding laundry for a family of four (7-9 loads a week)	2 hours for 9 loads	1 hour for 6 loads

Multiply the 2 hours it takes to fold nine loads of laundry by 52 and you get 104 hours, or 4⅓ days a year. After clothing is streamlined, your folding days are streamlined also—down to 2 days a year.

Now combine the Before figures—17⅓ hours to sort clothes plus 4⅓ days to fold clothes—and our total is more than 5 days a year spent on sorting and folding laundry! However noble and necessary these tasks may be, wouldn't you want to do them in *less* time if possible?

So far, considering only dusting, vacuuming, and laundry, you've spent almost 12 days a year working in a cluttered, overloaded environment. If streamlining can cut this time in half, thus saving you almost 6 days a year on these three chores alone, think of the time and energy it can save you on the myriad of other home management tasks you regularly perform. You can see why we say this system gives renewed "home managing hope," and why journalists say we "give new meaning to the term 'Environmental Protection'!"

MORE SPACE

We live in an affluent and materialistic society. Radio, television, magazines, even books all tell us that possessing things makes us successful, important, attractive, and happy. But few of us have the space, mental or physical, to accommodate all that we've been inspired to collect. We all seem to acquire more than we need, and in the midst of that clutter, it's not easy to find the things that count (and we don't mean just material belongings). The solution: Find what's worth keeping and discard the rest.

Let's look in a typical kitchen gadget drawer, for example—that is, if we can get it open past the heads of the handmixer beaters and two wire whisks. We discover not only the beaters and whisks, but four potato peelers, two ladles (one of them rusty), several dull paring knives, and three pancake turners (two plastic ones and a metal one with a broken plastic handle). This isn't all. More digging unearths two tangled electric frypan cords, two sets of measuring cups (one plastic, the other dented metal), and two sets of measuring spoons. Wedged in among all these "necessities" we find five cocktail forks, one gooey, rusty can opener, four little plastic pop bottle lids, three rubber spatulas (two with ragged edges), and a bunch (we've quit counting) of Popsicle sticks.

This drawer definitely needs streamlining. We begin by discarding one wire whisk and three potato peelers. If you ever manage to round up four people who will peel potatoes simultaneously, you can borrow three extra peelers from a neighbor—who is certain to have them. The rusty ladle and dull paring knives don't deserve space in any drawer, so out they go, too. No one should have to use a pancake turner with a broken handle, and there are already two good ones, so why keep the broken third? The frypan cords—assuming they work and are for different pans—should be stored, wound and secured, with their respective pans. Keep only one set of measuring spoons and cups, storing them with the mixer beaters. When was the last time you used those cocktail forks? If it's been more than a year, toss them. And get rid of the rusty can opener at the same time; then replace it with a new one. Four plastic pop bottle lids, although small, add to the confusion; for simplicity's sake, group them together (assuming they are keepers), perhaps in a small plastic bag. (This goes for all small, like items—grouping them in small containers will keep them under control.) Finally, keep the good rubber spatula; throw out the two ragged ones. Obviously, this streamlining technique will create far more space in any kitchen drawer, and after this system is applied to the entire kitchen, you may even discover you're not nearly as short of kitchen space as you thought.

Finding more space is a priority for almost everyone today. By clearing out the clutter and overload, you will make your home not only look bigger but actually feel bigger. In fact, streamlining on a large scale might convince you that your entire house has the perfect amount of space for your family after all.

NO MORE CLUTTER

After you organize what is left from streamlining, and things are taken from their assigned spots, they can be put back quickly and easily—no more "chucking and stuffing." Now notice we said "can" be put back quickly and easily. We didn't say "will" be put back quickly and easily, because we must be realistic. Family members may come along and wreak havoc with your best-laid plans.

But the point is that now you at least *have* places for things; before streamlining you had no such hope. It *is* possible to reduce clutter and confusion. Now that things have assigned spots in your rooms, you can create order and long-term control of spaces and things. And when you need something, the chances of being able to go right to it are *greatly* enhanced. However, this still leaves us with the issue of the havoc-wreaking family members—which may seem hope-*less*. We haven't any brilliant insights to offer—just the same-'ol same-'ol . . . be persistent and consistent in what you're trying to do, and then after a year or two if they're still wreaking havoc, shoot 'em at dawn!

In the introduction we talked about the "place-for-everything-and-every-thing-in-its-place" advice as being unrealistic because we no longer have the luxury of enough places—if we keep EVERYthing. This advice has another flaw: It doesn't go far enough. When we thought about places and things to put in those places, our reasoning went like this: "The place for junk is in the junk drawer . . . the place for clothes is in the closet . . . the place for mixing bowls is in the kitchen . . . ." It turned out that we were trying to make a place for *tossers*, because we'd made no distinction in our minds between useful posses-sions and the junk we really didn't need, like, use, want, or have room for.

The place-for-everything adage is too broad and general as it stands, but if you do the streamlining first, it works. Ever since our Ah-ha Experience (de-scribed in the introduction), streamlining is our saving grace. Things no longer have vague or random placement in our homes, and we no longer waste pre-cious time "treasure hunting." Because streamlining left us with fewer items to organize, finding specific places for things and keeping them there have become easier. Under these circumstances, even a child can maintain almost any space in the home—and who doesn't need the extra help and bonus time that being freed-up would give you?

EASIER MAINTENANCE

If you streamline, you will have a home you can be proud of without spending all your time and energy keeping it up. Streamlining isn't magic, and no little fairies will do last night's dishes or mop the floors, but there *will* be less to do. Take kitchen counters, for example: Removing the items that used to sit on the countertops automatically eliminates that constant "wipe and shine" routine. Because appliances are out of the way of spills and spatters, they stay cleaner longer and require less attention, and you'll find the counters themselves will be easier to keep clean because there will be little or nothing to remove when wiping up. Another benefit of keeping your countertops empty is that kitchen helpers can clearly tell when they are finished with the cleanup.

MORE EFFICIENT LAYOUT

Spaces that hold too much stuff are not only ugly but inefficient as well. For example, a front hall closet is a better place to keep coats if they aren't made to ire with the vacuum cleaner, golf clubs, sleeping bags, and boardgames for space. And back to the kitchen countertops: They will invite you, graciously rather than demandingly, to cook or bake if they are free of the toaster, electric can opener, blender, canisters, Crock Pot, and food processor.

You are probably muttering with some hostility, "Oh sure, sure . . . so *where* do I put all this stuff?" Well, remember that streamlining not only assigns items to appropriate places within your home but also to charity boxes and trash bags. Trust us: There will be a proper place for everything that's left after streamlining.

A BETTER-LOOKING HOME

Managing belongings goes hand-in-hand with owning them. Part of the management is making decisions about the purpose of things and their place in the home. Constant decision making can bog you down, though. If you don't know where to put something, or if you're faced with a number of homeless items, you're likely to let each one sit where it is, or to cram it in somewhere it shouldn't go. Years of living with clutter and shuffling clutter have taught us that clutter isn't charming, pretty, or restful, no matter how attractive each individual component may be. But when every keeper has a proper place and is put there, each item will look its best and will function at its best. And that makes the entire home look better.

PEACE OF MIND

No matter where you spend your day, your home is the key to your world. Because even if you do something other than homemaking for a living, your home is also your business. If you aren't managing it well, everyone suffers, but *you* suffer the most—from low self-esteem, from anger at the chronic mess, from frustration over not being in control of things. And if you do work outside the home, it's likely that the out-of-control house affects your on-the-job performance and attitude. Research shows that if you're in control at home, you have a higher chance of performing up to your potential in your career. When the home-related causes of these negative feelings are eliminated, you'll feel a lot better about yourself, and that improvement will be reflected in everything else you do.

Consider the benefits in just one area—hospitality. No more qualms, psalms, or sweaty palms over an unexpected visitor seeing your house in its "real-life" state. No more frustration and fatigue when you're preparing for expected guests. No more envy and depression when comparing your house with your neighbor's. Having more space, order, a better-looking home, and efficient rooms that are easier to look after will take care of all that.

LESS STRESS

This goes hand-in-hand with peace of mind. Medical science tells us that human beings have a high need to be in control of situations. And when this control is missing, we experience a vague discontent, and absence of peace of mind, or stress. Think of all the things in your life over which you have little or no control and that cause you chronic stress: the IRS, the Dow Jones Averages, inflation, the National Debt, the weather, the arrival of Daylight Savings Time, grade school carnivals, who moves in next door, your wayward teenager, the price your mechanic charges to fix your car, a cantankerous co-worker, the cost of mailing a letter, and so on. While much of life reels out of control, it's a comfort to know there's at least one area of your physical world over which you can have *total* control—the world of your physical spaces and things.

Psychologists have found that to reduce stress, we should simplify our lives and eliminate the trivial. This is where streamlining fits in. Thanks to streamlining, long-term control can be achieved within one to six weeks, depending on your degree of overload and the amount of time per week you can devote to it. Being master of your home environment minimizes the stress of day-to-day living; it motivates and energizes you. You may even find that the elimination of some stress plus the addition of extra time and energy will inspire you to go on to conquer other weak areas of your life.

We challenge you to put our "streamline first" ideas to the test. Be open-minded, follow the instructions, and use the concepts faithfully for twenty-one days (it's been said that it takes three weeks to break a bad habit and establish a good one). We know when you trade shuffling for shoveling, you'll reap all the benefits we've described—and probably a few more.

TWO

BASIC TRAINING

Laws to live by and steps to take to achieve physical control of things

This book is based on five basic household laws that we've developed and tested in hundreds of homes. Through phone calls, letters, and visits, we've kept in touch with many of the home managers we've worked with over the years, so we know that these ideas still apply and work in their homes. The rules will work for you, too, no matter what size your family is or what your income level, or whether you live in the city, the country, or the suburbs.

Now let's take a look at the basic laws covered in this chapter:

- The law of household physics
- The law of household ecology
- The law of household reduction
- Three price tags
- Surface mess vs. surface neatness

THE LAW OF HOUSEHOLD PHYSICS

The Law of Household Physics says, "Only so much will fit into one space and still let you retain order and control." You can't cram 3 square feet of stuff into a 1½ square-foot drawer and expect that drawer to look nice or stay looking nice after you've plowed through it looking for something; and don't expect to find what you're looking for quickly and easily.

To keep everything in bounds, remember that the amount of space available is usually fixed; it's the amount of stuff that's variable. You must eliminate some things if you want permanent control of your spaces. That means either learning to live within the limits of your physical space or facing the constant frustration of living without control of that space.

THE LAW OF HOUSEHOLD ECOLOGY

It's easy to abide by the Law of Household Physics if you live according to the Law of Household Ecology: When something new comes in, something old must go out. This keeps a balance between things and space. When you get a new coat, get rid of that tired, less stylish one; stop giving space to it, hoping it will come back into style. Even if it did come back into style, which is perfectly possible, it still wouldn't look good because of the worn elbows, frayed pocket edges, and saggy seat. When you get a new ballpoint pen, throw away the old, dead one; stop sacrificing space to keep it, hoping it will be resurrected with a renewed filler. If you've decided disposable razors suit your needs, discard the dull-bladed, exhausted electric razor. In short, maintain a manageable balance by dumping something old when you bring in something new.

THE LAW OF HOUSEHOLD REDUCTION

Overload reduces the amount of living space in any home. The more things, the less space; reduce the things and you automatically expand the space. Remember that when you stop shuffling and start shoveling, you'll remove approximately fifty thirty-gallon-sized trash bags filled to bursting. You can imagine how much space this frees up. In fact, we've talked to many people who said that after streamlining, they found not only order and control, but what seemed to be a "new" home as well. Many who once complained about a too-small home are now content with their existing space.

THREE PRICE TAGS

When you're assessing your belongings, remember that everything has three price tags. The first price is the one paid at the time of purchase. After the item is brought home, you pay a second price, in space. Every thing you own, whether it's a bobby pin or a rolling pin, takes up *some* space. The third price is the cost of maintenance, which translates into a time and energy cost. Almost everything you own must be maintained in some way. So look at your current possessions and at any purchases you may consider in the future, and ask yourself if you really want to pay three times. Often, the initial monetary investment turns out to be the smallest of the three.

SURFACE MESS VS. SURFACE NEATNESS

There is an important distinction between these two surface realities. Surface mess is what you have when you're in the kitchen canning peaches and fixing supper at the same time. It's what you have in the living room when all the carpet area is covered with gift wrap, boxes, ribbons, and gifts, as you wrap the Christmas presents. It's what you have when every available surface in the office is stacked with reports, files, and notes, while you're trying to meet a deadline.

According to the Law of Household Reduction, when you decrease the number of things, you expand your space visually as well as physically.

Surface mess isn't a problem if everything in that mess is a keeper, has a specific place to go, and can be put there quickly and easily. Surface mess is a normal result of living.

Surface neatness is a problem, however. When you have surface neatness, you're likely to be doing the household shuffle—moving items (usually tossers mingled with keepers) from place to place—far too often. It's a phony lifestyle, and one that too many people are living. It's neat on top only, and temporarily

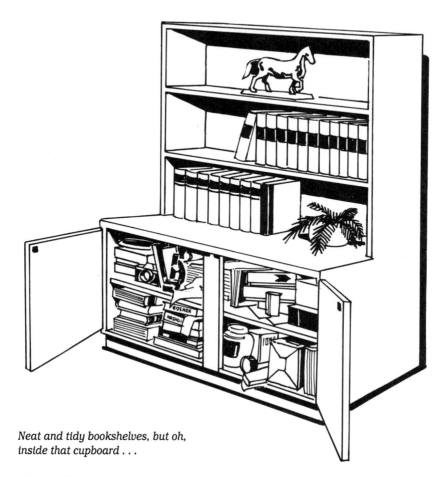

Neat and tidy bookshelves, but oh,
inside that cupboard . . .

at best. It's what you have when you know you're expecting company and you hope they don't open the wrong door or cupboard. Surface neatness is self-defeating, because it isn't the complete picture.

The real story is in your home's skeleton—in its closets, cupboards, and drawers. The condition they are in tells the truth about what shape a home is in. The skeleton is healthy if it has been streamlined down to the bare bones. Then the surface neatness syndrome is eliminated; there will be little or nothing that can escape and wander, and you'll have an easy time with clutter control.

EIGHT STEPS TO CONTROL

Part of the basic household laws and another facet of Basic Training are our eight steps to control. Now that you're convinced sorting out and streamlining

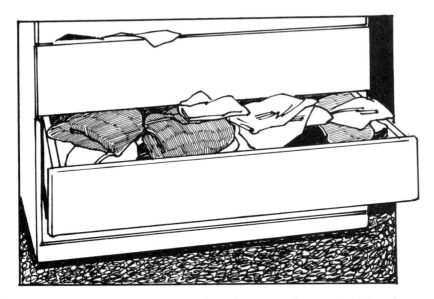

Drawers are part of a home's skeleton where clutter control is essential. When drawer contents are out of control, not only your household skeleton, but your entire life seems unmanageable.

your family's belongings really *will* make a big difference in your day-to-day life, let's team up your determination with the following step-by-step plan:

- ✔ Step 1: Prepare your family.
- ✔ Step 2: Collect containers.
- ✔ Step 3: Work in a clockwise pattern.
- ✔ Step 4: Evaluate and assign.
- ✔ Step 5: Ask the right questions.
- ✔ Step 6: Group and store like items together.
- ✔ Step 7: Use treasure boxes.
- ✔ Step 8: Enjoy the empty space.

STEP 1
PREPARE YOUR FAMILY

Tell *all* members of the household what you're planning to do, how you will do it, and why you want to do it. For example, tell them (1) you're planning to decrease the amount of physical belongings in the home and empty out some spaces; (2) streamlining is the method you'll use, which means you will get rid of everything that isn't liked, used, needed, wanted, or that there isn't room for; and (3) the reason you are doing this is obvious—you're tired, frustrated, and nuttier than a fruitcake from living in and maintaining an overloaded house. If you reassure everyone that they won't lose the things they *do* like, use, need, want, and have room for, they may be less resistant to the whole idea. But if your reassurance doesn't work, tough beans! Forge ahead anyway.

Make sure everyone understands what they can expect from you, and what you will expect from them while you're digging out from under the overload. Maybe they can count on you for meals and clean laundry. Certainly they can expect you to be exhausted and drained at the end of a streamlining day. And family members should know that they may be called on to haul out filled bags and boxes, to move furniture, to give extra help with chores, or to just stay out of the way. Since you will not be making decisions for older family members (teenagers and up), these people may also want to pay attention to what's going on. It's almost a sure bet they will eventually want their areas of concern (bedrooms, personal bathrooms, and so on) to look like and be manageable like the rest of the house. They will be the ones to make decisions about their own junk, so they will need to understand the system. At any rate, since family is most likely part of the problem, a clear and thorough orientation to what's coming will enhance the chances of their being part of the solution.

STEP 2
COLLECT CONTAINERS

This may not be a new concept, but it definitely works. You'll need four big containers per room—large boxes, heavy-duty trash bags, even brown grocery bags. Label one "Someplace Else" for any keeper that doesn't belong in the room you're working in. Label another "Charity" for usable things that you no longer want or need anywhere in the house. If you itemize deductions on your income tax return, you can ask the charity for a receipt when you drop off your tax-deductible donations. A more efficient way to do this is to supply a complete list of the items you're donating, with their estimated values. Then charity staffers can initial and stamp the paper you provide. Label a third "Garbage." Be discriminating when you load charity bags—much of the stuff people send to charity really belongs in the garbage. Label the last container "To File." You'll find filable material in all parts of your home. (For example, Alice found her family's life insurance papers in a master bedroom dresser drawer.) The To File box or bag should catch everything from misplaced insurance papers and birth certificates to appliance warranties, your eighteen-year-old's first essay, stray photographs, and even newspaper and magazine clippings. Group all filable material together, but don't deal with it until your entire home is streamlined; then you will have the time and mental energy to conquer your files.

Don't take time to go through the Someplace Else containers until you've sorted out the whole house (you'll get sidetracked otherwise), and brace yourself for the temporary mess that they can cause. You'll be accumulating lots of

Use containers such as these to gain order and control during the streamlining process.

them, and you will wonder where everything will go. Of course, you'll have little trouble with the charity and garbage items as their destinations are a given. It's the collection of "someplace else" things that could cause you some panic or irritation. Just remember this: While you're piling up Someplace Else boxes, you are also emptying space. Eventually all these things (only keepers, remember) will fit into the empty spaces you've left in each room. To avoid potential stress and frustration, set aside an out-of-the-way holding spot (a room, large closet, garage corner, or against a basement wall) as a temporary catchall for the Someplace Else bags and boxes so that you're not tripping over them as you work through your home. We call it a *temporary* catchall because it will be; each and every "someplace else" item will be dealt with by the time your streamlining is over. So be patient with the mess.

To avoid confusion, tie the charity and garbage bags differently—maybe twist-ties for the garbage and yarn for the charity bags. And do yourself a favor: Don't allow anyone to open a closed bag or box. Family members will set you back two weeks and undo every good thing you've accomplished by playing the "I Can Use This" game with you.

Now for the small containers. There's no set number. Just collect lots of shoeboxes, plastic refrigerator containers, cottage cheese and margarine tubs, drawstring bags (see our streamlined drawstring bag construction idea which is in the Back-of-the-Book Bonuses section), and so on. Shoeboxes, for instance, can be used in dresser drawers to hold folded underwear, socks, pantyhose, rolled belts, and so on. The plastic refrigerator containers and cottage cheese and margarine tubs might hold hair ornaments, paper clips, sewing notions, cookie cutters, and so on. Drawstring bags can be used to hang up all sorts of things that ordinarily would take up shelf or drawer space: makeup, toys, ski goggles, hats, gloves, extra bars of bath soap, razors, tubes of toothpaste, and so on. You'll use these containers to gain order and control of the interiors of closets, cupboards, and drawers by grouping similar categories of small things together.

STEP 3
WORK IN A CLOCKWISE PATTERN

Work in a clockwise pattern around the perimeter of each room, bringing your four big containers with you. Working like this enables you to see where you've been and know where you're going. This method also prevents time-wasting distractions. If you are in a bedroom, start at the closet. Deal with *each* item you come to as you progress around the room, assigning things to the four containers. (Moving in a clockwise pattern is a good technique when cleaning, too.)

Follow a definite pattern as you go from room to room, also. If you've begun in the master bedroom, work clockwise through the house from there. If you have a multilevel home, proceed clockwise around the floor you start on before moving to the next floor. Save the kitchen for last. It's always a big job, and time consuming. You will be glad to have the experience of streamlining the other rooms under your belt before you tackle it.

STEP 4
EVALUATE AND ASSIGN

Professionals in any business are always evaluating processes, products, personnel, procedures, inventory, and so on. A professional home manager does the same thing. (And a professional home manager isn't necessarily a full-time one . . . just one who is always looking for a better way to do things and is thorough on the job.) Think about *where* things are used and *how often*, as well as *when* you use them and *why* you use them. Answers to these questions determine appropriate resting places for everything. The shoeshine kit is a good case in point: If it's used often, then it deserves convenient storage space. And if it is used in the kitchen, then it should be stored there, rather than in the bathroom, bedroom, or basement. The turkey roaster is another example: Although used in the kitchen, it is used only seasonally, so it doesn't deserve prime kitchen space. It would be better to store it in some out-of-the-way place and take it out only when needed.

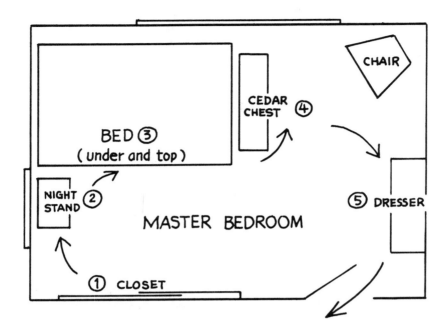

Begin streamlining in the master bedroom, starting at the closet and moving clockwise from one area to the next.

Have you ever thought about what you want on the right-hand side of the top shelf of your front hall closet or what you specifically want in the bottom drawer of your bathroom vanity? Or what would definitely work best in the top drawer to the left of the refrigerator? Start thinking this way: Assign specific purposes to all spaces in your home and then allow them to fulfill those functions and none other.

Not only does this evaluating/assigning technique make you more professional in your home managing, it puts rhyme and reason into the physical spaces of your home, thus eliminating the chucking-stuffing approach to putting away. No longer will you stuff those three extra packs of toilet paper into the vacant spot on the shelf of the hall linen closet—that is, unless this space has been given that specific assignment. Using this step alone will stop the creep of clutter and save you much time and energy.

STEP 5
ASK THE RIGHT QUESTIONS

This is the key to making efficient storage decisions. Before storing anything, ask yourself the following questions for each item in each room.

✔ Do I like it?
✔ Do I use it?
✔ Do I need it?
✔ Do I want it?
✔ Do I have room for it?

Even if you answer yes to the first four questions, if you answer no to the last one, you may need to reevaluate. The key to gaining permanent control of your home is to work *with* your space, not against it. Remember the Law of Household Physics: You only have so much space, and sometimes there just is not enough room for all that you like, use, need, or want. It may come down to a choice between lots of stuff and little control or less stuff and lots more control. Remember that keepers *plus* tossers create overload. Keepers by themselves don't do that—rather, they add individuality to your home.

Be ruthlessly realistic when deciding what to toss and what to keep, and think quality over quantity. Do you really like that all-cotton tablecloth that needs laborious ironing each time it's used? Is it really safe to use that heating pad with the short in the cord? Do you really need those wooden skis that you haven't been on in twenty years? Do you really want that white straw purse with the cracked bamboo handle? Asking yourself all five questions about everything you own will make letting go of things easier, create "new" space, and help you stop shuffling things around. So get into the habit of thinking about your things. Make these questions and their answers part of your lifestyle and your approach to home management.

STEP 6
GROUP AND STORE LIKE ITEMS TOGETHER

Again, this isn't a new idea, but it's very important. Doing this will put logic into the placement of things. Notice how almost everything in your home fits into categories: sports equipment, stationery and office supplies, grooming aids and appliances, yard maintenance equipment, games and family entertainment items, and so on. By mentally categorizing your physical possessions, you complete the first step to storing them. The second step, then, is to decide where each category of items should be stored.

This rule includes storing seasonal items—such as snowsuits, boots, and gloves—together and out of the way when they're out of season. It's wasteful to give these things prime space all year round. (When you've finished streamlining each room of your home, you'll be ready to put order into your storage area once and for all—whether this is the basement, a separate room, or a garage corner. We discuss this in Chapter 15.)

The practice of grouping and storing like items together has several advan-

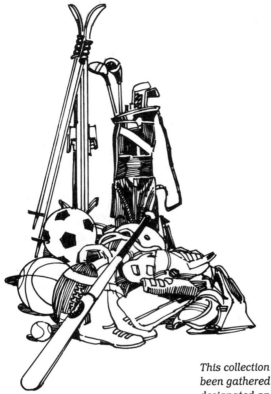

This collection of sports equipment has been gathered together and is awaiting a designated and appropriate storage spot. Storing all like items together helps everyone know where to find things—and where to put them away.

tages. First, you will have only one place to look for things. Second, finding and putting away becomes easier as you put a stop to the household treasure hunt pattern. Third, children can efficiently and responsibly help put things away. Fourth, you can now put things away without "away" being full to the brim of all kinds of things that don't belong there. Finally, grouping and storing like items together is a great time, energy, and nerve saver. It lets you know what's missing and what's duplicated. It buys you space and creates order.

STEP 7
USE TREASURE BOXES

There is a place in our homes and lives for the sentimental. According to author and household management expert Daryl Hoole, that place is a memory or treasure box. A cardboard orange or apple box with a lid from the grocery store

A treasure box solves the problem of storing sentimental treasures.

makes a good starter box, and each family member should have his or her own. We suggest that you eventually invest in a good quality container—perhaps even one that's custom-made—with a hinged lid. Ideally, your treasure box should be as nice as the contents, an heirloom in itself.

Baby books, scrapbooks, photo albums, heirlooms, vacation mementos, a last doll or treasured toy, and baby booties are some content suggestions. Large manila envelopes (one for each family member) could hold report cards and selected school papers.

Obviously, this isn't something the neighbor children are allowed into. A treasure box is not a toy box but rather a central holding spot for the child's personal treasures. Memory box items mean nothing to the neighbors; thus there is a strong chance these treasures could be abused, should uncaring hands get hold of them. Assign this box to the child's closet shelf, where it will be available, but just enough out of reach to ensure protection.

As a child moves from one stage of development to another, his idea of "treasures" changes. One month he's into G.I. Joe guys, six months later his treasure is his baseball card collection, and eventually his interest moves from his baseball cards to his school yearbook. Note that the child's contributions will also share space in this box with your additions—the baby album, first rattle, bronzed baby booties, and so on. So, to prevent this box from expanding to the size of a ministorage unit, have your child occasionally reevaluate the box's contents, discard some things, and make room for new "treasures." This is excellent experience; it's a lucky child who learns early on to live the Laws of Household Physics and Ecology.

STEP 8
ENJOY THE EMPTY SPACE

The principle of empty space is a design element that's been used for centuries, and it's a basic part of your home. It is peaceful, airy, calming, even beautiful. Empty spaces visually open rooms up, making them feel bigger. Any realtor will tell you that if you are trying to sell your home, you should empty out and clear off some spaces (end table tops, fireplace mantel, piano top, corners of the room, and so on) to get better results. Empty spaces visually tidy rooms up. Even if you haven't dusted or vacuumed for a few days, if the clutter is removed and some empty spaces are visible, the room will look and feel cleaner.

Make empty spaces a home management standard. Just as a bathroom isn't clean until the chrome is shiny, so the cleaning of any room shouldn't be finished until some space is emptied. Work to keep a little empty space in every room of your home. Alice's kitchen is the size of a phone booth, yet she has an empty drawer in there. In case this sounds slightly nutty, let us explain. Our prestreamlined days were so frustrating, so chaotic, so stressful, that the very *thought* of ever slipping back into the old way of living causes panic and cold sweats. We realized we needed some sort of constant reminder that would keep us on track. Thus the "keep a little empty space in every room" advice. It is our signal, our proof, that we are now in control of the stuff—it is no longer controlling us and never will again!

Don't let empty space make you nervous. Don't succumb to the primal urge to fill it up, just because it's there. It does take some getting used to, since it's almost always a radical change (before, every windowsill, countertop, corner in any room—*any* surface, nook, or cranny—was filled to bulging). We're not advising that you waste space; rather, we're asking you to value it, work to keep it, and allow it to be *your* signal and keep you on track, too. So give empty spaces a chance for twenty-one days, and you'll end up loving them even more than your filled spaces.

Overloaded and out-of-control space is exasperating and depressing.

Enjoy empty space and the feeling of control.

SOME FINAL ADVICE

Now that you know what *to* do, here are a few *don'ts.*

- ✔ Don't be afraid to get rid of things.
- ✔ Don't feel guilty about getting rid of things—or wanting to.
- ✔ Don't keep anything that is broken and cannot be repaired or that in your heart of hearts you have no intention of repairing.
- ✔ Don't allow well-meaning givers to intimidate you into keeping things you really don't want to keep. Many of us worry that so-and-so will "just die" if we get rid of her gift. Experts agree that no one dies when we toss something out that was given to us. Rather than let your spaces fill up with things you don't want, like, use, or need because of this guilt business, hold on to the *feelings* that came with the gift instead. Make it a

constant practice to distinguish between things and feelings, and you'll play it safe when it comes to future overload.

And remember, this major cleaning out is a one-shot deal. If you consistently live by the Laws of Household Physics and Ecology, continue to evaluate and assign, group and store like items together, and maintain empty space in each room, you'll never have to dig out like this again. Adopting these steps as part of your lifestyle will ensure this. So let these eight steps become your home management standards; they will change your life.

THREE

ON YOUR MARK, GET SET . . .

Getting your household transformation off and running

T here are some things you and your family should know before you start your household revolution. The most important thing is to realize in advance that it won't happen overnight or without some strain. We all know that to be successful in any undertaking (playing a tennis match, taking a school exam, running a marathon, making a public presentation, or streamlining a home), some mental as well as physical preparation must take place. This chapter is devoted to getting you ready emotionally for the big changes you'll be making.

Expect to be tired at the end of each streamlining session. This is hard physical work, so you might want to consider ordering out for dinner, especially on the day or days you do the kitchen. Or treat your family to a meal at the nearest fast-food place. And because you'll be physically and mentally exhausted when you finish each streamlining bout, be sure to pamper yourself a little (a hot, perfumed bubble bath, some time with your feet up and your favorite book, or even a bottle of Perrier and some soothing music). It is in large part because of this exhaustion that the first of the eight steps to control was to prepare the family—make sure your family understands they can depend on you to perhaps provide meals and clean laundry during this time, but little else.

Brace yourself for some family resistance. Bad habits die hard, and we've seen that many families feel threatened by this change in their lifestyle. They can cope fairly well with the picking up and putting away, but the throwing and giving away cause anger and sometimes opposition. After all, their identities, personalities, and very lives are intertwined with their belongings. After we helped streamline a neighbor's master bedroom and kitchen, the homemaker's spouse would shake his head and moan, "My assets, my assets," every time he saw us. So let them have their delirium tremors, just don't let them wear you down. Stick to your guns!

Learn to let go. Count on experiencing some emotional strain yourself. Misplaced sentiment can make it hard to let go of things. One friend of ours, whom we helped dig out a closet, was giving precious space to more than a hundred pounds of stained, stretched-out, faded baby layette items. She knew she needed the space those items were taking up; she knew most of those things were beyond ever looking nice again; she knew she'd be able to replace them if she needed to. But none of that made disposing of those items any easier. She cried, but once she had discarded the stuff, she was glad she had.

How's your attitude? Part of your preparation will probably involve an attitude overhaul. Basically, our attitudes about belongings, not the objects themselves, cause overloaded houses. These attitudes can restrict, even cripple you, as you struggle to keep order in the home. For instance, if you're firmly convinced you can't get along without your junior prom dress from 1969, your square-toed platform shoes, and your polyester double-knit floor-length skirts, then you won't give them up. And if you won't give them up, you'll continue to live and struggle with overloaded closets.

We've helped thousands streamline their homes, and without exception, this is what we heard: "I can't throw that away, I might need it someday," or "My mother [or sister, or husband, or neighbor] would just die if I got rid of this!" or "Get rid of that? No way! I paid good money for that!" Then there's: "We're gonna get this fixed someday," and the real zinger, "We're saving this for so-and-so." (Believe us, so-and-so will be better off if you don't save it for her.) If you are thinking or saying any of these things, an attitude overhaul may be in order.

An attitude overhaul will cut your streamlining time by two thirds and save you energy. Case in point: The kitchen of a 1,950-square-foot tri-level home took nine and a half hours to streamline (and the home manager had emptied all the cupboards and drawers before we arrived!) because a lot of time was spent talking her out of things and into new ideas. We not only had to deal with her belongings but her preconceptions and closed mind as well. In contrast, the kitchen of a 2,000-square-foot ranch house took three hours to streamline. And these three hours included the time it took us to help the home manager unload all her drawers and cupboards. This woman was open-minded and receptive to all of our basic principles and steps; all we had to deal with was her *things*. So speed the project up and save lots of stress and energy by keeping an open mind and a positive attitude about the changes.

Streamlining your home involves lots of good changes. Be flexible enough to try something different. Professionals in any field are always looking for a better way to do things; they're frequently changing this arrangement or that system. Instead of saying, "How can you have an empty shelf?" or "There's not enough room for this anywhere else!" or "There's no other way to do it," be professional in your outlook, and give yourself the freedom to experiment and make changes.

Prepare for potential stress. Not only does getting rid of items cause stress, but decision making does, too. Brace yourself for it. Streamlining requires hundreds of decisions, all made by you. When we were helping one home manager streamline her master bedroom, we found an assortment of more than seventy-five greeting cards in her bottom dresser drawer. She had to decide what to do with every Mother's Day card, birthday card, anniversary card, and all the get-well cards she'd received for her 1959 tonsillectomy. She was definitely becoming stressed. After looking at about twenty-five cards, she put five or six in her treasure box, picked up the rest and said, "What's the point in keeping all this? Why did I do this to myself?" Then she dumped the whole bunch into the trash. She had learned some important concepts from this exercise: You can't afford to give valuable space to nonessential duplicates, and finding appropriate places for all potential keepers causes you to be very selective in what you keep. It's this selection process that will head off potential stress in the future.

Deal with doubters. Be aware that some of your acquaintances may greet your bubbling enthusiasm over your new home management style with a lack of interest and/or with distrust. Don't let this hurt or discourage you. Disinterest, even mild ridicule, are common reactions when people sense progress or success in another's life. And you'll definitely be progressing and succeeding as you take control of your physical surroundings. Just be prepared for this reaction, chalk it up to human nature, and continue in your enthusiasm for the project.

Lay the groundwork. Streamlining goes more smoothly if there has been some schedule coordination, too. Clear the calendar as much as possible. Decide how many of your activities and responsibilities can be delegated, canceled, or postponed. Even if you're in a position where you never have large, unbroken blocks of time at home (as is the case for anyone working outside the home), clear the calendar as much as you can and do the job a little at a time. Folks have devoted their days off, even vacation time, to pursuing this quest—it was that important to them. Having four part-time jobs and twelve children between us, we know firsthand what it's like to be exhausted and short on time. Yet we also know that the exertion and sacrifice necessary to achieve a streamlined home are truly worth it, because we couldn't even keep our heads above water if we weren't living in and managing streamlined homes. Whatever *your* at-home schedule is like, you'll appreciate a simplified schedule during this project, so take deliberate steps to control the demands on your time until you've finished.

On the day of "overload attack," put your family on alert. This is courteous and helps ensure their cooperation and involvement. Again, since they are most likely part of the problem, you'll need them to be part of the solution. Because streamlining involves much change, apply all the positive psychology you can to ease them into it. (It's been said the only person who likes change is a wet baby.) Again, reassure them that nothing will be tossed out that is needed,

JANUARY			Goal: Streamline house			
SUN	**MON**	**TUES**	**WED**	**THURS**	**FRI**	**SAT**
		1 *holiday*	2	3	4	5 *Streamline M.Bdrm (baked chicken)*
6	7	8	9	10	11 ←*Streamline 7-10 bath*	12 *line→ guest rm (lasagne)*
13	14 ←*Streamline 7-10 Kids rm (pot roast)*	15 *7-10 hall closet (spaghetti)*	16 *7-10 family rm (fish/chips)*	17 *7-10 Kitchen (Soup+Salad)*	18 *7-9 Kitchen (go out)*	19
20	21	22	23	24	25	26 *Streamline Storage (hamburgers)*
27	28	29	30	31		

Plan ahead. Clear your calendar as much as possible so you will have undivided time to concentrate on streamlining.

used, or dearly loved. Discuss the quality versus quantity idea, and your desire to raise the entire family's standard of living.

In the case of small children, you won't want them underfoot as you do their rooms (send them off to school, to Grandma's, to the neighbor's, or wherever), not only because of the demands they make on your time, but because they will want to keep everything you decide to toss, thus slowing the process to a turtle's trot. You may also want to inspect their freshly streamlined rooms each morning before they go off to school or play, to encourage consistency with the new habits.

Teenagers and spouses, reluctant or willing, are another story. They should be taught the system and allowed the autonomy to deal with their own spaces and possessions. There is always someone in our seminar audiences who is anxious to try this system but whose reluctant or negative spouse is stonewalling the whole idea. We have some tried and true advice for all of you who are "saddled with hitches-in-your-git-along": Ignore them. Streamline your specific areas of responsibility (*your* side of the closet, *your* share of the dresser drawers, *your* night stand — and, in all reality, probably the rest of the house, excluding teen bedrooms) and ignore the overloaded and self-defeating spaces of your naysayers. Meanwhile, diligently and consistently keep up your areas of concern. It won't be long before these doubters understand that you are not simply off on another "toot," as in times past, and that this change is lasting and for real. Your improved disposition and higher energy level, coupled with a consistently sharp-looking and well-managed home, will in time convince them that they're missing out. We've seen it happen hundreds of times—eventually the negative family member comes around. Have faith and carry on!

Finally, be sure they see and feel your positive attitude, enthusiasm, and seriousness about this project and your desire for improvement. Express your faith in their ability to change and your appreciation for their promised cooperation.

Gather the necessary supplies. This will be your last bit of preparation. These supplies will cost you little or nothing. You'll probably be able to use what you already have on hand.

Here's what you need:

- ✔ Assorted containers for storage, give-away, and throw-away items
- ✔ A dark marking pen for labeling boxes, bags, and cupboard containers
- ✔ A permanent laundry marker for marking all children's play clothes labels
- ✔ Yarn for tying up the charity bags (The bags with twist-ties will have a different category of contents from the bags tied with yarn.)
- ✔ A small box with index cards in it for recording contents and locations of all storage boxes. For instance, your keeper Christmas or Hanukkah decorations will be put in a numbered container. On an index card with a corresponding number, you'll list each item in the box, then indicate its storage location. (See illustration.) This idea also applies to those who use their personal home computers to store their records and household management information. You truly will have storage at your fingertips. The benefits of this routine are many: You hunt through only a card file for your item, rather than the entire house, saving time, energy, and wear and tear on nerves. You also have at your fingertips an accurate, ready inventory of all stored belongings. Thus, if you're considering purchasing a new Sunday dress for Susie, you can check your card file or computer screen to see if you already have an appropriate dress in her size. (Remember, for anything to be a keeper and worthy of saving and storage, it must be in top condition.) Under this system, your storage areas work for rather than against you. No longer is there the possibility of storage areas becoming "lands of no return."
- ✔ Paper and pencil for listing items that need to be purchased later (Each room usually needs a few things to help it meet its potential.) If you carry

BOX 21 — under stairs
1 - two sets popsicle makers
2 - Soccer uniform (size 6)
3 - two girls swimsuits blue (size 10)
4 - Girls shorts (size 6-14)
5 - boys swimsuits (red size 8 blue size 10)
6 - b[...]ts (size 4-12)
7 - [...]'s swim towels

[...]X 6 — garage
1 - Christmas twinkle lights
2 - Christmas yard lights
3 - tree stand
4 - one bottle tree preserver
5 - tree skirt
6 - Christmas stockings

Storage at your fingertips is a benefit of using the card-file system.

this want list with you when shopping, you're less apt to forget what you need. It's smart to give copies of the family Wants and Needs lists to grandparents and other gift-givers in your life. Doing so increases the chances that you and your family will receive things that are truly liked, needed, wanted, and used, and lessens the chances of future buildup of potential charity items.

Someone once said, "There is no chance, no fate, no destiny that can circumvent, or hinder, or control the firm resolve of a determined soul." This has certainly been true for us and thousands of other home managers across America, and it will be true for you, too. You're determined, and now you're prepared, so adopt this creed as your own, and . . . On your mark, get set . . . go!

KAREN'S ROOM

wants:	needs:
① new stenciling	① new lamp shade
② new bed-spread	② carpet cleaned
③ matching curtains	③ dresser handle
④ shelf	④ bulletin board
	⑤ framed mirror

You should have one "Wants and Needs List" for each room you are streamlining.

FOUR

MASTERING THE MASTER BEDROOM

Bringing restful order and simplicity to your bedroom

Accocording to author and interior designer Alexandra Stoddard, many of us spend an average of twelve hours a day in our bedrooms: tidying up, dressing and undressing, arranging our wardrobes, exercising, reading, reflecting, sewing, writing, puttering, sitting, talking, listening to music, observing the weather, planning, watching television, playing with a child, loving, daydreaming, nursing a cold, eating meals on a tray, napping, or truly sleeping. It is possible you might spend half your life in this environment. So the master bedroom should be the most special room in your house. It should be beautiful, a private sanctuary. Because it's an adult retreat, it is the place above all other rooms where peace and order can reign.

Stoddard maintains that this room should suit *you* and suggests you concentrate on making your bedroom all you wish it to be. It needs to be serene and pretty. Details are important; you want your eyes to fall on nourishing things—your spirit needs this and you deserve it.

Because you begin and end each day there, it has more of an influence on you than any other place in your home. Self-esteem starts here, first thing in the morning, every morning. Seeing that this room is under control and lovely will make a big difference in how each day starts.

Despite its importance, the master bedroom in many homes doesn't get the attention or affection it deserves. Often, it's the last room to be decorated. In her book, *Living a Beautiful Life*, Stoddard says, ". . . over the years, I have found that in many homes, the master bedroom has been one of the most neglected rooms in the house, a room that has been badly misunderstood . . . . It's worthwhile to put your energies [and money] into getting this room to feel right, *first*—and *then* reach out and create rooms for public view."

After several years of in-home consulting, we have come to the same conclusion. We've seen this room serve as the unofficial storage bin for the whole house. Clean laundry, unsorted and unfolded, covers the bed; magazines litter the floor; tennis rackets hide in the closet; general clutter and disarray are the order of the day.

Even if things are not quite so bad at your house, there are several good reasons to start your overhaul with the master bedroom.

- You'll need an orderly, under-control place to retreat to when you work on the rest of the house.
- A successfully streamlined master bedroom will serve as a motivator and energizer while the rest of the house is deep in clutter.
- This room very likely holds a large percentage of sentimental things. That may make for some psychological barriers to the clean-out process, but once you've surmounted them here, you'll be well prepared to deal with the rest of the house. Doing the master bedroom first is like going through boot camp—it's tough, but it prepares you for anything that follows.
- After your dresser and closet are streamlined, you'll no longer be wearing out-of-style clothes, too-tight clothes, too-big clothes, or otherwise unflattering clothes. (An added plus—you'll probably find that others show you greater courtesy, respect, and attention when your dress consistently reflects self-respect and pride.) And delving into a dresser drawer where socks are tucked neatly inside themselves and nested by colors in containers, and where only stockings in perfect condition are to be found, will really make you feel good.
- Cleaning a streamlined bedroom gives you a sense of control and accomplishment, too. In a streamlined bedroom, you can vacuum the closet floor and even under the bed. (That's home management supreme!)

Now that you're convinced, here's what to do.

CLOSET

In any room that has one, the closet is the place to start. Use the key questions— "Do I like it? Do I use it? Do I want it? Do I need it? Do I have room for it?"—to evaluate every little thing in there. Start with the clothes rod. Don't worry about getting rid of too many clothes. Speech experts report that only 7 percent of the real meaning in a conversation comes from the actual words that are spoken. The other 93 percent of the total meaning comes from nonverbal messages— mostly from appearance. You can see, then, how important it is to present a sharp appearance. Therefore, when dealing with clothes, keep your standards high: Quality over quantity is the watchword.

In her book, *Dressing Rich*, Leah Feldon states that quality is a condition of excellence and that in fashion this implies the highest standards of design, fabric, and workmanship. Unfortunately, quality—in all aspects of life—is a rare commodity these days. Author Feldon explains that products are developed and marketed to appeal more to the taste of the middling masses than to the taste of the most discerning . . . and that makes for a lot of junk out there. Leah Feldon's bottom line is that "Worn quality looks better and richer than perfect junk." She goes on to say that a small, flexible, and select wardrobe composed of top-quality apparel is one hundred times more effective – and easier to manage – than a colossal collection of mediocre clothing. We, as your Clutter Therapists, say AMEN!

"You don't need a new and different ensemble for each day of the year, or even for each day of the week. It's not a stigma to be seen in the same outfit more than once, even if you are constantly in the public eye. If anything, it is a demonstration of self-confidence, security, and fashion wisdom," says Feldon.

Therefore, don't hang on to anything that's too small – you know, the things you're saving for when you lose weight. When you do lose weight, you'll want and deserve new, up-to-date clothes anyway. And speaking of clothes and weight gain, noted educator Dr. William Purkey claims, "You're not getting bigger, clothes shrink while hanging in the closet – it's the dark." So get rid of that load of unworn, sad-looking clothing and you'll enjoy your eventual new purchases more. (Did you know that the average person wears 20 percent of his or her wardrobe 80 percent of the time? As you scrutinize your collection, you'll probably realize this is true for you.) Your favorite pieces are out front, within easy reach. The things you never wear are pushed to the back and may even have a little dust across the shoulders at the hanger line.

CLOSET CLEANING TECHNIQUE

You might want a friend to help you with your clothing decisions. An outsider's objectivity could speed the job along. Take out only one thing at a time, and don't keep anything you think you'll make over. Chances are, your unfinished projects list is long enough right now, so you don't need to add anything more to it. (Old denims are legitimate keepers if you sew. The versatile, classic fabric has so many more lives than just jeans – bat and ball drawstring bags, hats, campsite pot holders, even picnic quilts, for example. But remember, only if you will actually use these old blues should they be kept. Wishful thinking doesn't count any more here than anywhere else!)

Establish a keeper pile of clothes as you fill the charity and garbage bags. Your keeper pile ought to be much smaller than the charity and garbage piles. When you rehang the keepers, group like items together for both an orderly look and greater efficiency. For instance, hang all shirts together, hang all slacks together, hang all jackets together, hang all dresses together. Break up suits and hang each element with its counterparts – skirts with skirts, jackets with jackets, and so on. Also, it's a great idea to group like colors together within categories.

Don't overlook the usefulness of inside closet walls. They're good places to hang purses, belts, ties, a lint brush, and so on. You'll find you don't need anything elaborate for this hanging business—finishing nails, screw-in hooks, or plastic hooks with the adhesive backs work well.

Work on the closet shelf next. There's something about a closet shelf that seems to shout, "Things, things! Give me your poor, your tired, your wayfaring things!" Don't listen. Your shelf will do just fine and you'll like it better if you clear everything off except your treasure box, an extra blanket or two, and possibly a few hat boxes. If there's no other place to store your boxes of out-of-season clothes, you'll find your closet shelf an accommodating place to do this, now that all the unrelated clutter is gone.

Now go to the floor and deal with the shoes. Whether you put your keepers on a rack, in boxes, in a shoe bag, or just line them up on the floor makes no difference. Just make sure you keep only quality and avoid duplicates (do you *really* need three pairs of old, worn out tennis shoes or black pumps?). Don't give valuable space to dead shoes.

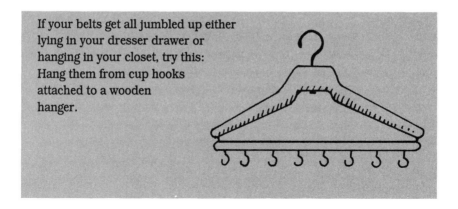

If your belts get all jumbled up either lying in your dresser drawer or hanging in your closet, try this: Hang them from cup hooks attached to a wooden hanger.

Shoes stop looking "right" once they reach a certain age. To ensure a fresh, stylish look, buy high quality shoes (preferably all leather) to start with; pay particular attention to the look of the toe and to heel height and heel thickness; note the visual weight of the shoe sole; avoid flashy, faddish looks. The platform shoes of the seventies are a great example—extreme in every instance—and believe us, they will *never* return, so quit saving them!

Footwear experts say shoe styles usually have a two-year to three-year life cycle. The first year a style emerges is considered the fast side. The third year in the life of this style is considered the slow side. Buying on the fast side enables you to get your money's worth out of your shoes; you'll look stylish longer, and therefore you'll want to and be able to wear the shoes longer.

In *Dressing Rich*, author Leah Feldon tells us that to look best, boots must be kept proportional to our total outfit. For instance, boots are generally too heavy to be worn with a silk dress. No matter what the fashion magazines are showing, Feldon warns, "short boots worn with skirts or dresses are deadly for most women. Also, avoid a space between the top of your boot and hemline."

For better boot storage, clip each pair at the top to a skirt hanger and hang, either from the clothes rod or on the back closet wall, below skirt level, from a nail or hook. This takes care of the boot flops. (Be sure to wipe the heels and soles before hanging to prevent dirt rubbing against walls or clothes.)

When you're deciding how many pairs of shoes you need, remember what professional wardrobe planners say. They suggest you plan your wardrobe around two basic, harmonizing colors, then choose two or three pairs of shoes to match your wardrobe color choices. It's not necessary to have a rainbow-colored fleet of shoes.

One category of clothing you may wonder what to do with is the trendy and faddish. Remember, legitimate fashion is influenced by and is a reflection of socioeconomic conditions. In *Dressing Rich* we're told that trends and fads are most often spawned either by a big, immediate push from the fashion industry or by a highly publicized media event like a movie. *Tom Jones, Doctor Zhivago, Annie Hall,* and *Urban Cowboy* are a few examples of movies that exerted an influence on fashion. "Some of the more unappealing faddish items that I have noted within the last few years are the jumpsuit, which is at its best when being dropped from an airplane; high-heeled backless sandals, which are especially tacky when worn with tight jeans or bathing suits . . . Jellies, the clear plastic flat shoes . . . and the newly revised jodhpur pants . . . ," says Feldon. We would add to this list the miniskirt and, for men, the polyester leisure suit and the Nehru jacket. So what to do with trends and fads? Number one, if you have them, either put them in your children's costume box or get rid of them. But *don't* give them any more precious closet space. And number two, wise up — don't buy any more!

> Clothes will look fresher and last longer if hung on soft satin or velvet padded contour hangers. Wire hangers often leave lines and sometimes ruin the drape of the garment.

If you have permission to enter what is often "no man's land," move to your partner's side of the closet and handle it like yours. If you meet with resistance, remember our advice to consistently set a good example by keeping your own areas of concern streamlined and orderly; then be patient.

By the way, twice a year, when temperatures and seasons change, sort through your clothes and eliminate everything that is no longer useful to you. Designer Stoddard, in *Living a Beautiful Life*, advises you to get rid of things that no longer fit you, your current needs, or your sense of personal style. She says results are best when you try everything on in front of a full-length mirror. Stoddard explains that this twice-yearly ritual will save you daily time and confusion and make it more likely that the things you wear will flatter you now and make you feel attractive.

From *Living a Beautiful Life*, by Alexandra Stoddard, comes this advice: Buy clothes staples—stockings, underwear, and so on—twice a year (preferably on sale) to avoid wasting time. When you find the right kind, invest.

When the closet is finished, continue working in a clockwise pattern around the room, taking your four big containers with you. Confront the next item or area you come to.

DRESSER

Let's say your next stop is the dresser. Try to narrow down its function in your mind before you do anything else. This will help you empty and refill it properly. If you've decided it is to be used for certain categories of clothing, then out go the medicine and cosmetics, the hidden chocolate chips, the tube of tub-and-tile caulking, the orphaned keys, the expired credit cards, the "who's-this-a-picture-of?" photos, the treasure box items, and everything else that landed there because you didn't know where else to put it.

Work with the dresser as you did the closet, touching and assessing one thing at a time. (You may have the impression as you read this that this is a laboriously slow process. It is. But only for the first little bit, while you're in the closet. After you have worked like this for a while, you get the knack, you see the end result in your mind, and you pick up steam.)

Don't keep old, yellowed slips or stretched-out bras (and don't save the hardware; you aren't going to reuse those hooks and you know it). Don't save worn-out underwear—believe us, there's zero chance its tired elastic will resurrect into new, snappy stuff, no matter *how* long you keep it. Get rid of all torn nylon stockings and threadbare socks. Toss out discolored, exhausted jockstraps.

Speaking of nylons, here's how to keep those delicate accessories protected and under control: Hold the pantyhose at the waistband; fold them in half, lengthwise, placing one leg on top of the other; while still holding the pantyhose by the folded waistband with one hand, use your other hand to bring the toes of the stockings up to meet the waistband; next bring the knees up to the waistband; continue folding the nylons up to the waistband until you have a small bundle, three to four inches long. Finally, fold the outside, sturdier tummy panel over the leg bundle, just as you fold a pair of crew socks together, by inserting your thumbs inside the outer layer, folding it down over the leg parts.

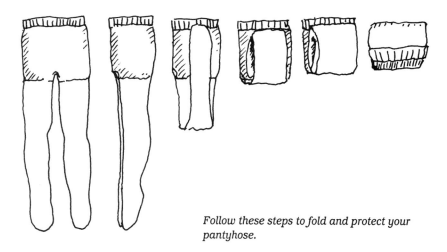

Follow these steps to fold and protect your pantyhose.

Here are some useful dresser tips:

- Use small containers, such as shoeboxes, inside the drawers to hold groups of things: bras, rolled-up nylons, scarves, belts (if you don't hang them in the closet), crew socks, pocket things (such as keys, spare change, notes to self, pocketknife, wallet, pen and pencil, and so on), underwear, and so on.
- If you share a dresser, assign the top drawer to your partner. Put a small box inside to hold all the pocket things listed above. Then, if he should happen to clutter the dresser top with these items, you can simply open the drawer, and sweep it all into the drawer container. Presto! A clean dresser top.
- Fold full slips and place in the drawer with the lace hems showing.
- Fold panties and underwear also, so that they fit neatly into a small container.
- Fold two-piece items, such as pajamas or sweats, together by folding the bottoms over the folded top (this is a consolidation idea).
- If the insides of your drawers are wooden, try spraying them lightly with a favorite cologne or environmental oil before adding your drawer liners. It's a luscious experience to open fragrant drawers.
- Keep the dresser top clear except for two or three attractive items, such as a houseplant, nicely framed photo, dresser lamp, potpourri, candlestick, and so on. A minimal number of decorative accessories will look nicer, expand your space visually, and make dusting easy.

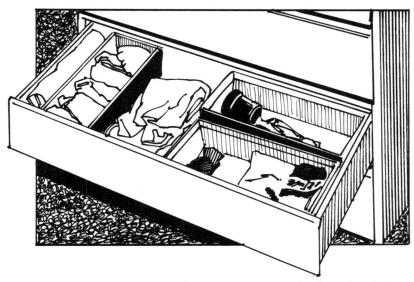

Using containers inside a dresser drawer gives permanent order and control.

- Don't leave the dresser until you've made definite assignments to each drawer, it looks nice, and you're happy with it. Change things around and experiment until your new system works for you.

UNDER THE BED

Dig it out, then keep it empty. There will be enough room throughout your home to accommodate all the keepers from under your bed. So leave this space clear; it's easier to clean and it's a constant signal that you are in control. We've streamlined the smallest of homes, even single-width mobile homes, and we've always found better storage in other areas of the home. Try doing without under-bed storage for twenty-one days. If you're still not convinced, go back to storing under there, but at least do yourself the favor of dividing this area into quadrants (top left, bottom left, top right, bottom right). Then give each quadrant specific assignments, and group like items together. Some categories of items that store well under a bed are spare sheets and blankets, out-of-season clothes, luggage, even a treasure box (if it fits). Don't forget to make a storage card (or log this information onto your computer storage list) with the heading "Under Master Bedroom Bed" and itemize what each quadrant holds. Giving your under-bed space specific assignments will not only save you time when looking for things, it will save your back, too.

There is one valid exception to this "no under-bed storage" rule, however.

This is the platform and waterbed with built-in storage drawers. Deal with this type of storage as you do your dresser drawers, using small containers to hold groups of like items together. These drawers could also house spare sheets and blankets or out-of-season clothes.

NIGHT STANDS AND BEDSIDE TABLES

If you are absolutely sure you need one or two of these, then deal with them ruthlessly because they can be real clutter boxes. Maybe your night stand's purpose is to hold a lamp, a clock radio or alarm clock, the phone, or all three. If there is a drawer or shelf, maybe this could hold the phone book and your journal or daily planning book. But basically it ought to be clear and kept that way, for the same reasons as the dresser top.

WALLS

Even though we all deserve beautiful, high quality furnishings in our homes, what we deserve and what we have can be two different things. So while we are setting goals and making plans to get what we really want, let's use what we do have with style and flair.

Walls are great places to add some style to a room. If your bedroom walls are plastered with eight years' and four kids' worth of grade-school vintage Mother's Day and Christmas presents, then assign the most precious to your treasure box, hang the latest arrival(s) on your laundry area wall (this soothes the feelings of the giftgivers and brightens a usually drab spot), and throw the less meaningful away. You might even take a picture of the child holding the gift she gave you, then discard the item itself.

As you're deciding what to do with your walls, remember to watch out for the trendy look; the country look of stuffed teddy bears and stenciled wooden accessories may be cute, popular, easy-to-do, and inexpensive, but does it say anything specific about *you*? After all, this special room should radiate your personality, not that of the local craft class leader. Your own tastes, heritage, and background are a rich resource for decorative ideas; use these as inspiration for design statements about you.

Be careful, too, of visual clutter. Too much of anything is just that—too much. It's not tasteful or enhancing. Don't let empty wall space intimidate you. Interior designers work it into the decor because of its restful, space-expanding effects. So do your best to keep your walls elegant and *simple*. (For a detailed lesson on correct picture placement, see Chapter 8, "The World's Window on You: The Living Room.")

CEDAR CHEST AND OTHER EXTRAS

Sometimes a cedar chest is the place for treasures. Whatever it holds, deal with each and every item inside it. Keep only positive things that bring warm memories and make you feel good. Then, once it's loaded with keepers, deal with the chest itself. If it isn't attractive in its own right, maybe it could go into a behind-the-scenes storage area. After all, everything in your master bedroom should reflect your taste, style, and quality. If there is an item that doesn't do that, consider removing it.

Watch the general furniture overload in this room, too. You can visually open a room up by removing some furniture. Don't let your bedroom be a dumping ground for extra furniture that you don't know what to do with. For example, Alice removed an office desk, her sewing machine cabinet, an old cedar chest, and a chair from her average-sized master bedroom. All this overload had shrunk the bedroom down to nothing. But she found other places for all the items; the room looks twice as big now—and much better. If your room is small, you might think about putting your dresser, chest of drawers, or cedar chest in your closet.

One last tip: The best way to stop furniture encroachment and to decide which furniture pieces will and won't go in any room of your home is to first determine the specific purpose(s) of the room. Give every room in your home a specific assignment (or two or three or . . .) and then allow that room to fulfill that function or functions and none other. A sample list of room functions will illustrate what we mean:

ROOM	FUNCTION
Master Bedroom	Sleeping, TV viewing, reading, letter and journal writing, napping, dressing, exercising, grooming, chatting on telephone
Living Room	Conversation and entertaining, TV viewing, reading, game playing, napping, and piano practice
Family Room	Hobbies, telephone chatting, plus the same things as the Master Bedroom and Living room (except for grooming and dressing)
Kitchen	Eating, food preparation, conversation, game playing, homework (if the table is there), canning, and using the telephone

Laundry Room	Sorting, washing, and drying laundry, mending, ironing, polishing shoes, caring for houseplants, even cutting hair

If you're still not convinced of the importance of this room in your life, here is one final thought from interior designer Alexandra Stoddard: "The mood you create in your bedroom holds great power of association; it can become a self-portrait of your past, your present—who you are now—and it can give you a taste and vision of the personal journey that lies ahead." Always remember to keep your standards high and choose the best for yourself, and as you continue to "master your master bedroom," it truly will become the most special room in your house.

FIVE

BRAVING THE BATH

The keys to sparkling, efficient bathrooms

N obody loves a bathroom. In fact, our surveys of over two thousand people have shown this room to be the least favorite room in the home, because it's hard to clean and it gets grungy so quickly. But nobody wants to do without one, either. In fact, the higher the ratio of baths per person in your household, the better. But even having enough bathrooms to go around doesn't always mean any or all of them will be in the condition you'd like them to be.

Regarding the condition of this room, interior designer Alexandra Stoddard says, "Everything in our surroundings speaks for us, and if we accept living with a vulgar design we must pay for it. Caring about aesthetics increases our sensitivity. The more we care about the small details, the more in tune to beauty we become, and the more we realize how seemingly insignificant items affect us . . . . Take care of every inch of your surroundings . . . let your eyes wander. [We] get enormous pleasure and comfort from orderly, harmonious, attractive surroundings, and [we] feel unhappy and disturbed when things are out of place . . . . Train yourself to see things with caring perception."

Therefore, to achieve beauty and order in this room, look beyond hygiene, grooming, and sanitation to what this room is *not,* because the more cluttered a bathroom is, the less efficiently it will perform its designated tasks and the less chance you have of creating a lovely interior. It is *not* a storage room, a library annex, a beauty supply or pharmaceutical warehouse. It *is* usually a small room with minimum space for anything other than the bare (!) essentials. It doesn't usually lend itself to housing backup supplies of toilet paper and so on. So start streamlining each bath in your house by first searching it for storage overload.

The basic purpose of this room is grooming and hygiene. At the risk of sounding redundant, we repeat: The more cluttered the room is, the less effective it is for these tasks. As you evaluate the drawers, cupboards, and space under the sink, you'll probably find many unrelated things stored (or shoved) here and there. Curling irons, hair dryers, and hair grooming accessories such as combs, ribbons, rubber bands, and bobby pins are stuffed into drawers or onto shelves that you must dig through each time you need something. Or a bathroom drawer is so overloaded that hairbrushes roll in the stray squirts of toothpaste, and toothbrushes gather lost strands of hairbrush hair. And wallowing among all this may be missing puzzle pieces, lonely pennies, or orphaned Fisher Price Little People. We've seen cupboards and under-sink areas stuffed with towels, bed linens, and unrelated miscellany. We've found the toilet plunger, loads of cleaning supplies, and a toilet brush buried under a pile of dirty laundry.

Survey the countertops, the top of the toilet tank, the windowsills, and the corners of the tub. More than likely you'll see the makings of a small drugstore, with an inventory of hairspray and deodorant cans, shampoo, bubble bath, perfume bottles — even plants. Weed out some of this stuff so the maintenance will be easier, the space will visually expand, and the total view will be lovelier. Then find places to store your daily grooming products — the shampoo and cream rinse, the shaving cream and razor, the bath powder and lotion, and so on. Your goal will be to put these things as close to their point of use as possible without their being out in the open. Your bedroom closet shelf, a dresser drawer, and a hall closet shelf are a few possibilities if you have no bathroom vanity or other bathroom storage. To make an inconvenient situation bearable, you'll want to organize this stuff into a carrying caddy if you must keep DAILY grooming supplies in *another* room. While we recognize this advice may sound unrealistic, we still give it as the best alternative to tripping over and cleaning around collections of "parked" toiletries.

Work to keep surfaces basically clear and you can keep them clean. And after your major streamlining, develop the habit of weeding out the excess three or four times a month. As you add your personal designer touches, remember to keep only a few quality objects in sight. (Be strict with yourself or you'll end up with another pile of clutter.)

THE VANITY

Our streamlining step of "Evaluate and Assign" works especially well with cupboards and vanity drawers. Any vanity, regardless of size, serves you better if its contents are assigned to specific spaces. This will stop things from drifting and scattering.

Drawers: If your vanity has drawers, you're lucky. Some drawers will need smaller containers installed for grouping similar small items together. A drawer assigned to hair accessories will be fun to get into when all barrettes, rubber bands, combs, clips, Victorian bows, and so on are in their own containers. If you must make more than one assignment per drawer, be sure you group like

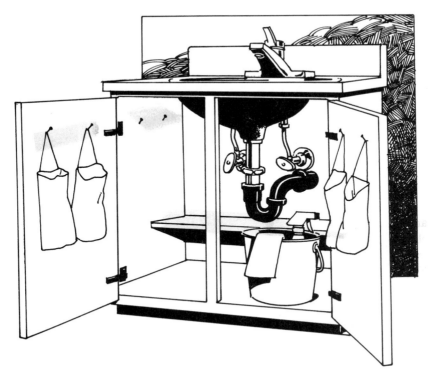

A shelf and finishing nails multiply under-sink storage space in a vanity.

items together in small containers. For a finishing touch, spray the insides of each drawer with an environmental oil or your favorite cologne and line each drawer with a pretty floral paper.

Under the sink: Lots of possibilities here. First, expand your storage space by installing a shelf in the back, under the pipes. Second, insert hooks into the underside of the vanity top. Third, insert hooks or finishing nails into the inside vanity walls and on the inside of vanity doors. What's being stored under the sink determines how far apart your hooks and nails are. Fourth, consider painting the interior of this space a white or off-white high gloss enamel to brighten it up and make cleaning easier. We know people who have laid Formica (a remnant piece, cut to fit), on the floor of the cabinet. Again, this is another touch that makes maintenance easier, plus it adds protection in the event of a leaking pipe.

The shelf in the back is a good place for an extra pack or two of toilet paper, a cleaning bucket, the plunger, or the toilet bowl brush and holder. Whatever you put on the back shelf, remember that it's somewhat hard to reach, so don't assign things to it that you need three or four times a day, such as a container of combs and brushes. Incidentally, there's nothing sacred about the length of a plunger handle. If yours has a long handle, saw four or five inches off; then it will fit nicely under any sink.

From the nails and hooks you inserted, you could hang the curling or crimping iron, blow dryer, and drawstring bags. Drawstring bags are among the neatest things around — they efficiently utilize ignored and wasted space. Use them to hold extra toothbrushes, feminine hygiene needs, hair clippers plus attachments, a few bars of soap, even your makeup if there is no other place. You'll think of a dozen more drawstring bag ideas. (You may want to label the bags — or make them out of different fabrics — so you can easily tell what's inside them.)

The vanity floor could hold a wicker basket, a large juice or shortening can (covered in pretty adhesive paper), or even a new clay flower pot for combs and brushes. This is the place for a cleaning bucket containing your bathroom cleaning tools and supplies. For your convenience, you'll want a cleaning bucket with duplicate tools and supplies under the sink in each bathroom in your home. If you're concerned about your toddler's safety, secure your cabinet doors with Kinder Locs, childproof locks available in hardware and discount stores. Try to keep the vanity floor as clear as possible, though, to make it easy to clean. (See illustration.) You'll find if you diligently practice the Law of Household Physics here, this space will serve you well, as it will remain efficient yet never full.

Vanity top: Keep it as clear as possible, with only a minimum of your lovely decorating accessories on display. Keeping the top clear will open up the room and expand your space visually. A clear top is much easier to clean, and when that's the case, you'll create a "reasonable cleaning opportunity" for your children. We all want and need our children to help with the upkeep of our homes, and if your spaces are simplified and surfaces are clear, you can look for and expect their help.

SHELVES, CUPBOARD, CLOSET, MEDICINE CABINET

Here are more storage areas that you want efficient rather than full. Storing all keepers in labeled containers will encourage efficiency. Toothbrushes do not need to sit in a holder on a vanity top. After all, you will pay a maintenance price for that holder. Consider putting the holder under the sink, inside a cupboard or medicine chest, or group the brushes into a tray-type drawer organizer.

If you're interested in eliminating some laundry loads and recapturing some space, don't stock these areas with linens. Instead, practice our "No-Linen-Closetology." (See Chapter 11, "Cabinets, Closets, Cupboards.") Assign each bathroom a certain towel color and each family member his or her own towel and wash cloth. You might add lace, eyelet, or monograms for easier identification. (Each family member is specifically identified by some device, such as towel color, lace, eyelet, or a monogram.) You may want to record this "bathroom code" and post it somewhere handy until people are used to this system and have memorized their designation. Put an extra set or two of towels in the cupboard or drawer for guests or emergencies, and box up the best of the rest to go into storage. Bring these towels out when the ones currently in use wear out. If you have any "on-the-way-out" towels, pair them up with all the swimsuits in the family. With a laundry marker, label each swim towel, then box up these suit-towel combinations for storage, too.

Now you have good family towels and washcloths hanging on your towel racks, each to be used by its respective owner (yes, maybe two or three times in a row), until you launder them. Then they're taken off the rack, laundered, and put back on the rack the same day. There is no medical evidence anywhere that says it's gross or unhealthy to use the same bath towel two or three baths in a row. And believe us, this technique *alone* will save you much time, energy, and money in the laundry room.

If there is any disadvantage to this idea (other than the difficulty of trying to convince your family to go along with it), it's that these towels may wear out a little sooner. But we're convinced the space this system buys and the definitely lighter laundry loads are well worth the trouble.

NO STORAGE (NO VANITY, NO SHELVES, NO . . .)

We've lived with this, and it's tough but not impossible. Again, living the Law of Household Physics helps. Minimum spaces dictate the need for minimum stuff. So the first step in coping with a storageless bathroom is to pare down to absolute essentials as if your sanity depended on it.

If you have a partner's shaving and grooming gear to worry about, deal with that first. Assuming there's at least a medicine cabinet in your bathroom, store gear in it. Then come the grooming aids: toothbrushes, toothpaste, antiperspirant. A typical medicine chest won't hold much more, so your makeup, in a container, will go someplace else as mentioned earlier — the corner of a dresser drawer, part of your closet shelf, or in a drawstring bag hanging on your closet wall. Consider keeping your good set of tweezers in an unidentified, only-you-know-where place, far from the set your children use, for obvious reasons.

All remaining bathroom inventory will also go someplace else, such as on a closet shelf or in a cupboard in either the master bedroom or hall closet. Use a set of tiered hanging wire baskets to hold a different category of things per tier. Even a small wicker trunk under the sink, if there's room, could accommodate these items. No more hiding the cracked tile and the mold growing along the tub ledge with the bubble bath, shampoo, and conditioner. No more using the windowsill and top of the toilet tank as makeshift shelves. If there's a shower head, a shower caddy is a legitimate need and will keep some of the items out of the way. But overall, get rid of the visual clutter and the maintenance drudgery by putting your keepers someplace else.

DIRTY LAUNDRY

Does your bathroom look like a hurricane just hit, with dirty clothes and towels strewn all over? Carelessly tossed laundry creates tremendous irritation and inconvenience. To improve this situation, make a specific place for dirty laundry. When there's a designated spot for dirty laundry, the responsibility for keeping it picked up rests flat on family shoulders.

If you use a laundry hamper, consider giving it up. Hampers are space eaters, and most bathrooms have little space to sacrifice. They must constantly be moved for floor cleaning. They get smelly, and even the most expensive can look tacky after a while.

If you don't have a slick system for laundry, try this: Buy or sew a hanging closet laundry bag for each person in your household. (See "How To Make a Closet Laundry Bag" in our "Back-of-the-Book Bonuses.") This solution is inexpensive and takes little space, and the bag can be washed as needed. Now we'll admit that in all realism, the average kid probably isn't inclined to actually carry his dirty laundry from the bathroom to his closet laundry bag. In fact, the average kid probably isn't inclined to even lift the bathroom hamper lid and drop the dirty stuff in. When you get right down to it, the average kid isn't inclined to do much, except eat, play Nintendo, and ride her bike. Does this mean we lower our hopes and expectations of children helping? No sir! As long as we create realistic and reasonable circumstances for them to function in, we are within our rights as parents to expect kids to pick up after themselves. So go for it—and don't get discouraged if desired results are slow in coming. If you're persistent and consistent, they'll come.

MORE BATHROOM BRAVADO

Bath toys. When it comes to children, what's a bath without toys? But don't get carried away: Allow only certain toys to be played with in the tub. And provide a drip-dry storage container, such as a nylon or plastic mesh bag, that the bather can hang up from the shower head or caddy when she's through with the toys.

The bathroom versus teens. Teenagers need it as simple as a four-year-old—but this need is complicated by the fact that they have and use much more grooming paraphernalia than a four-year-old does. Combine this "necessary" overload with the hectic schedules they keep (meaning there's no *time* to put anything away, anyway), and you have the recipe for a lost cause. For instance, they can handle tossing the blow dryer into a drawer or drawstring bag, maybe, but don't count on them to wind and secure the cord. So if you want your teen to help maintain the bathroom order without weeping, wailing, and gnashing of teeth, keep this room SIMPLE.

Bathroom scales. One of life's recurring minor annoyances is tripping over the bathroom scales. To avoid this, stand them up against a wall, put them under the sink, hang them on the inside of a cabinet wall, but get them out of the way.

First aid supplies. A few minor emergency supplies, such as bandages, petroleum jelly, tweezers, rubbing alcohol, hydrogen peroxide, and so on, can be stored in the bathroom if you have a secure place. Keep the larger, more extensive kit in a high cupboard, above the refrigerator, or on a high shelf in the hall closet. Discard old medicines; store the keepers where they are taken and out of children's reach. Group like items together in a labeled container.

Guest bath. If you are fortunate enough to have a guest bath, or even if you just want to welcome an occasional guest, here's a nice idea. Group a good set of towels, new toothbrushes, toothpaste, fragrant bath soap, hand and body lotion, disposable razor, shaving cream, and shampoo together in a drawstring bag or pretty basket. Bring this out when company arrives—you'll feel like a gracious hostess and they will appreciate the convenience and your thoughtfulness.

JANITORIAL DUTY

Remember that at the beginning of this chapter we said most people dislike this room because it's hard to clean and gets grungy so quickly? The bad news is, the gets-grungy-quickly problem will probably be with you until the grunge-makers leave home. But here's the good news: The hard-to-clean problem is solved when you brave the bath the way professional janitors and custodians do. Following is advice borrowed and adapted from professional custodian Don Aslett and his delightful book, *Is There Life After Housework?*

Step 1: Gather the tools and supplies needed for your cleaning bucket. The bucket itself can be any large plastic container, such as the type ice cream or laundry detergent comes in, or a standard mop bucket. This container will hold an old toothbrush (for scrubbing the hard-to-get-at areas, such as around the faucets, and so on), a plastic pot scrubber or nylon-covered sponge, and a professional window squeegee. (STECCONE is our favorite and is available at janitorial supply houses. These come in all sizes—small for mullioned windows to gigantic for picture windows and every size in between. This is the same squeegee professionals clean skyscraper windows with.)

The cleaning bucket also holds a cleaning cloth, which is simply a terry hand towel that's been folded in half along its width and sewn down the long edge to form a tube. (See illustration.) This cloth is far heavier and more serviceable than the old worn-out, ratty-tatty undershirts or diapers typically used for cleaning. And when this terry tube is folded in half twice, you have four cleaning squares on one side, and four cleaning squares on the flip side, as shown in the illustration. When this total of eight cleaning squares is dirty and saturated, simply turn the tube inside out, refold it twice, and you have eight more fairly dry, clean squares ready to go to work for you.

The remainder of the supplies to go into your cleaning bucket are two plastic spray bottles (quart size is best). The first bottle will hold highly diluted ammonia water. By highly diluted, we mean a *capful* of ammonia (sudsy or nonsudsy, it doesn't matter) to a quart of water. This mixture is used to clean windows and mirrors. You don't need an expensive blue-colored or foamy cleaner or one containing some mystical, magical ingredient to create a potent mirror and window cleaner. Highly diluted ammonia water is what the professionals use, because it's inexpensive and does the job. The second bottle will contain diluted hospital disinfectant. (Pine Odor 5 and Springclean are two excellent brands available at your local janitorial supply house. They run approximately seven to ten dollars a gallon but, because they are heavy concentrates and will be greatly diluted, will last about ten to twelve months.) This mixture is used to clean all porcelain fixtures, the vanity top, and the backsplash. We even mop our floors with it. Be sure to label each spray bottle so you don't get the two cleaners mixed up. Never use the hospital disinfectant on mirrors, as it will cloud and streak.

Step 2: Clean the mirror. Spray the mirror with ammonia water (allow the cleaner to sit for a second to break down the gunk), then take a swipe across the mirror top to eliminate drips and drops. Next, vertically swipe and wipe with the squeegee, wiping the rubber blade on your cleaning cloth between swipes, and proceed across the entire surface. If done correctly, there should be virtually *no* smudges or streaks—thus eliminating the need for the wadded-up newspaper, shiny-shiny ritual. But if by some chance you do end up with a streak, simply run your finger down it. The ammonia water removed the oil from your fingers, so doing this will not leave a smudge.

Step 3: Spray the sink bowl, faucet, vanity top, and backsplash with the hospital disinfectant. Again, allow it to sit a few seconds to break down the gunk and scummy buildup. This spray-and-wait routine is one that all professional custodians follow. It's called working smarter, not harder, by allowing the chemical to do the job it was created for—breaking down and loosening buildup.

Step 4: Rough up the scummy buildup in the sink using the plastic pot

scrubber or nylon-covered sponge. Run *no* water—this would eliminate the disinfectant benefits. Use the old toothbrush to loosen the gunk on the faucet and hard-to-get-at areas around it. When all scummy buildup has been roughed up, shine the fixture with the dry cleaning cloth, wipe the sink bowl and rim, wipe the backsplash and vanity top—all the while turning to a fresh cleaning square as you proceed.

This procedure saved you time (it took only two to three minutes), energy (the cleaner did the tough job), money (it cost just pennies per bottle compared to dollars per bottle of grocery store cleaners), and of course water (you didn't use any). It also saved your fine surface finishes since no abrasive cleansers were used.

The tub and toilet are cleaned the same way, using the disinfectant, the pot scrubber, and the cleaning cloth. An exception would be the addition of some toilet bowl cleaner when needed. (The hospital disinfectant is not formulated to tackle the toilet bowl.) And be sure you run *no* water.

One last professional tip: If you want to save even more time on bathroom cleaning, alternate the spray, loosen, and wipe process. In other words, after you've sprayed the sink and vanity top, go to the tub and spray all surfaces of it as you wait for the chemical to work on the sink and counter top. When the tub is completely sprayed, go back to the sink to loosen the gunk and wipe everything dry and shiny. Then, before you loosen the tub gunk and wipe it out, spray all surfaces of the toilet tank. While you're working on the tub, the chemical is working on the toilet. The toilet and tank are the last to be cleaned, unless the floor needs mopping, in which case you could spray the especially dirty areas of the floor and allow the chemical to work on the floor as you work on the toilet. When finished with the toilet, you could drop to your knees and, using the same cleaning cloth, mop your way right out of the room.

Again, this entire cleaning process is fast, easy, and thorough. The bathroom now looks beautiful, smells great, and is disinfected as well. Braving the bath the professional way might just make this least favored room downright tolerable.

SIX

CRIB NOTES

Starting off on the right foot
in baby's room

For baby's room to be a baby's room, the approach is basic: Get everything that isn't baby-related out. As clothes are outgrown, move them out; for safety as well as neatness, don't leave older children's toys in the baby's room.

CLOSET AND DRESSER

Babies need only a few pieces of dress-up clothing, and even these items rarely require closet space. So you can count on closet room to store things such as the playpen, walker, stroller, infant seat, even the diaper pail. Hang as much as you can, rather than stacking these things on top of each other on the floor. The closet shelf can hold one or two extra blankets or quilts and the baby's memory box, with the baby book in it. Don't overlook the many possibilities this space affords.

We know a young single mother in a one-bedroom apartment whose walk-in closet accommodates her baby's crib, thanks to some ruthless streamlining. With the crib along one wall, mom's and baby's basic clothing hanging on the rod opposite the crib, and their few remaining possessions (a suitcase, typewriter, and box of toys) tucked away under the crib, this resourceful mother created a suitable baby's room and solved a space-crunch problem as well.

With a baby comes a diaper bag. This is like the family car keys or mother's purse . . . it is easy to misplace if it hasn't been assigned a specific resting place. A suggestion: Hang the bag on a wooden hanger in baby's closet or on a sturdy hook in the closet wall.

If the closet seems like the best place for diaper storage, a hanging diaper organizer or stacker will help you. You'd be surprised how often we have seen clean diapers wadded up in a laundry basket in some remote corner of a baby's room. Plowing through laundry baskets is a time and energy waster, not to mention what it does to the room's appearance. If you use disposables, get them out of the bulky box and put them in a diaper organizer.

Be ruthlessly realistic as you streamline baby clothes and layette. Typically, sentimentality and frugality make it difficult to get rid of very much here, but don't give in to these forces. Toss out stained and worn clothes. Put good clothing that doesn't fit into a labeled box and into the storage area (see Chapter 15). Special pieces, such as a christening outfit, the cap and booties Grandma crocheted, a first pair of shoes, and so on, deserve a place in a child's memory box. Fold play outfits as separate units, tops inside the matching bottoms, and place them in a drawer; hang up dressy clothes. But remember: You will buy space and save on laundry time if you keep out only a minimum number of clothes.

Put containers in the dresser drawers for control. If there's space, put undershirts in one container, socks and booties in another container, plastic pants in another, all in one drawer. Put pajamas and sleepers there, too, if you have room. Play shirts, pants, and rompers could go in another drawer, and sweaters and outer clothing still another. What you are doing here is making rhyme and reason out of available dresser space by grouping and storing like items together. Any extra drawer space could be devoted to diaper storage if you prefer this to the closet diaper stacker.

OTHER FURNITURE

It's nice to have a rocking chair and a changing table in baby's room if there is space. But if you don't have enough space for the rocker, dresser, changing table, plus the crib, then make some choices. If the dresser is a low one, it can double as a changing table; or a standard-sized changing table can serve as a dresser. If you're blessed to be able to purchase new baby furniture, you'll find this very product on the market—a dresser and changing table combination. It's a great space saver. Also on the market is a crib/dresser/changing table combination that grows with baby. It eventually breaks down to separate pieces, with the crib converting to a small twin bed. One other possible solution to the space-crunch dilemma: Put the dresser or chest of drawers in the closet.

If baby hygiene takes place here, then put related supplies, such as powder, cream, lotion, cotton swabs, cotton balls, and so on in a container (those glorious shoeboxes. . .) inside a drawer for convenience. If there is no drawer space to hold these things, then perhaps they could sit on the closet shelf and be taken down as needed. We suggest you store nothing under the crib (unless yours is an extreme situation like that of our single mother mentioned earlier); you'll thank us when you vacuum.

To unclutter the room visually, get everything off those window sills. Remember, too, that your dusting and window washing will go much faster if you don't have to move the powder, lotion, and so on.

TOYS

An infant becomes a baby, a baby becomes a toddler, and on it goes. But a rattle stays a rattle, long after baby loses interest in it. So keep pace with baby's stages of growth and development – and keep toys rotated accordingly. Clear out anything baby is not currently using.

WHAT ABOUT SHARED ROOMS?

Babies' rooms are often small, if you're lucky enough to even *have* this room. So the most important point is: Keep it simple and easy to maintain. But how do you do this if baby must share her space with the sewing machine, an office desk, or even other people? Although in the introduction to this chapter we advised getting everything that isn't baby-related out, we also recognize that in the space-crunched world baby doesn't always have a private room. If that's the case at your house, divide the room up visually (or even physically with a piece of furniture or a partition) and make specific assignments to every space, nook, and cranny. Keep everything in the room in containers and allow only a bare minimum in there. Hang as much as possible. We can look to the Shakers for inspiration in making the most of our space. They used rows of wooden pegs along the upper third of their walls to hang anything that wasn't in immediate use – even chairs.

Roommates manage their spaces better if parents remove ownership ambiguity as much as possible – "This is Billy's shelf, this is baby's shelf; this is Billy's drawer, this is baby's drawer . . . ," and so on. Spaces may need labeling to aid the memory.

GOING SOLO

What about the lucky child whose room *is* his or her own throughout the stay-at-home years? Keep it streamlined during those years. The furnishings and decor should keep pace with the child's stages of growth and development. So don't store unused clothes, toys, games, furniture, accessories, and so on in this room. Assuming they are still keepers, move them to an appropriate storage area. When we start storing things in prime living spaces (bedrooms, bathrooms, and so forth), these spaces can take on a warehouse appearance. We all know warehouses are not comfortable or attractive. None of us enjoys sharing living space with storage. Very few of us can do this efficiently, and especially not children.

DECORATING DEVICES

How do you keep a baby's room simple yet stimulating? Try thoughtful application of bright colors, cheerful curtains, maybe a mobile above the crib, and some good wall decor in bright colors and simple shapes. Stenciling can do wonders. Or look to toddler coloring books for inspiration. Alice decorated an entire nursery wall with simple coloring book pictures. If you'd like to try this, section the wall off with painted lines, using masking tape as a straightedge guide. Then with a pencil draw a picture in each box. (If you don't trust your drafting skills, you could transfer the drawings by placing graphite paper underneath the picture, taping it all down, then tracing over the lines.) Finish it off by painting each picture with bright, washable acrylics.

While many vinyl wall coverings are bright and washable, the beauty of stenciled or painted decorating is its affordability, flexibility, and charm that only a personal touch can add. As the child outgrows the decor, it can be painted over and some other design applied.

You can repeat the theme by using the same technique on solid-colored, inexpensive fabric to be made into curtains. Section off the fabric using straight lines, then draw a picture in each space, using fabric crayons.

MOM ON THE RUN

According to Dr. T. Berry Brazelton, pediatrician and author, 52 percent of American women whose children are under three are in the work force. He states that these women have overwhelming demands made on their time and energy and must also cope with the guilt and grief experienced when they leave their children every day. Dr. Brazelton also notes that today's fast pace leaves the mom on the run with very little time to nurture both family and career.

With these thoughts in mind, we again make a case for streamlining the home interior. Living and functioning in streamlined spaces saves you time and energy and minimizes the stress induced by lack of organization. While we don't have a lot of little time-saving tips for the mom on the run (beyond our streamlining process), we do have one valid suggestion: Do as much as you can the night before to get yourself ready to leave the next morning for the sitter and work. For instance, prepare the diaper bag and place it with either the baby's coat or your coat, or put all three together in a designated spot. You might even have a separate set of toys meant only for the diaper bag and sitter.

Whatever you can do the night before to lessen the morning rush will be calming to you as well as to baby.

It seems our challenge today is to slow life down while still maintaining a competitive pace. We're convinced that keeping your home streamlined and consistently preparing as much as possible the night before is the secret to being serene rather than frantic while you're a mom on the run.

SEVEN

CREATING A KID-READY ROOM

Bringing order to kids' rooms

I n this chapter we'll discuss the young child's room as well as the teenager's room. Both rooms suffer from basically the same problems, and both are dealt with in basically the same way, but there are two differences—the age and interest level of the things involved, and who does the streamlining. *You* do the child's room; you *train* the teen to do his or her own room.

Maybe after years of struggling with the chronically messy world of youth, you've concluded it might be easier to just shut the door, make the best of the mess, and hope time will cure the problem (maturity, it's called). Don't give in to those feelings, and don't give up the struggle.

Your children need order; they flourish and thrive in it. Chores, such as cleaning their bedrooms, are an important part of a child's upbringing. Household jobs will help your kids master the mechanics of running a home and the skills needed for responsible living. And it all starts in their private world— their bedrooms.

The question, then, is what can you reasonably expect of a child? Family psychologist and author of *The Six-Point Plan for Raising Happy, Healthy Children*, John Rosemond, says your four- or five-year-old should be responsible for keeping an orderly bedroom and bathroom. He maintains that by age seven or eight, children should be responsible for daily upkeep of their own rooms and bathrooms as well as several other chores around the home. "Once a week, these children should be required to do a major cleaning of their room and bathroom. This should include vacuuming, dusting, changing bath and bed linens, and cleaning the tub, lavatory, and commode," Dr. Rosemond says.

While we heartily agree, there is something we must add: Asking kids to clean up a perpetually overloaded room is unreasonable—children can't cope with overload any better than you can (actually they do much worse, because immaturity works against them). But they try, shoving, cramming, hiding things here and there, hoping this time you won't notice what they've really done. You do notice, and they're in the doghouse. It's an eternal cycle, with no positive change in sight. But ask children to clean up a streamlined room, and you've found a reasonable task that's within their abilities. They deal with the minimum mess properly, you are pleased, and they are relieved. So break the negative cycle, lay the groundwork for a positive cycle to begin, and watch your children live up to their responsibilities at last.

Keep in mind that your primary goal in streamlining the children's rooms is to create a world that they can maintain mostly by themselves. Overload makes them avoid decision making when pickup time arrives; the less they have to deal with, the easier and quicker decision making will be. You also want the child's standard of living to be high. His or her room should look (and smell) clean, be attractive and comfortable, and radiate positive messages. First of all, assess the overall condition of the room, and if it needs it, make plans for improvement. It doesn't take any longer to maintain nice things than it does to maintain shabby, worn-out, tacky things. The same philosophy shared in the master bedroom chapter applies here: It should be a lovely retreat that inspires creativity and peace. So as you go about creating such a world for your children, be sure to use your paper and pencil to record the "wants" and "needs" for each room.

It is helpful if *all* the child's or teen's belongings are gathered into this room so you can get a full picture of what you have to deal with. Retrieve all dirty laundry to make sure it's all in the keeper category, and so you can more efficiently plan space for storing it when it is clean. If toys, sports equipment, art materials, books, and so on are scattered throughout the house, retrieve them also, and allow space for them in the bedroom, if possible.

A word on preparing the teenager: Use psychology. If she is handled right, she'll want you to teach her how and be anxious to do it. Don't press or nag; let her room wait while you do the rest of the house. She'll observe what is happening, see the results, and want the same thing for herself. Or you may prefer to bring in outside help; sometimes one of your friends can be more effective with your teen than you can. But above all, be pleasant, be patient, be persistent, and be consistent in the management of your areas of responsibility (your bedroom, the kitchen, the laundry area, the living room, and so on) so she has the benefit of your example to model.

Now you're ready to begin your clockwise pattern. This procedure is the same for both the younger child's and teen's room. First, make a sweep around the floor. As before, evaluate each item you come to, using the key questions. What doesn't go in the Charity, Garbage, Someplace Else, or To File boxes is a keeper for the room. Just as you did in the master bedroom, establish a keeper pile, somewhere in the room but out of the way. The things from this pile will "melt" into the room's empty spaces you create with your streamlining. After you have cleared the floor, begin working on the closet.

CLOTHING

After all the child's clothes are gathered, you'll probably have five categories of children's wear:

- Play clothes
- School clothes
- Dressy clothes
- Hand-me-downs (quality keepers that no longer fit anyone but will, eventually)
- Discards (those that go either to charity or the garbage)

Use these categories as you streamline. A child doesn't need lots of extra hardly-ever-wear clothing to keep neat and tidy, and you don't need them in your laundry each week. A child's basic needs include eight pairs of socks and underwear (one on, one in the laundry, six in the drawer). If you wash at least once a week, then he only needs seven play outfits and maybe one dressy outfit. However, if you're a mom on the run, working outside the home, and the laundry is left up to you, then perhaps a week's worth of these basics is not enough. You may want a few extra pairs of underwear and socks, and an extra play outfit or two, just as a cushion against getting behind in the laundry department. We also recognize that clothes are a VITAL part of a teenager's life and that they (especially girls) think they need TONS. So be it . . . as long as the TONS are made up of keepers *and* there are adequate places to house all of it. (Again, this is really up to your autonomous teenager.)

Separate keeper clothing this way: underwear, socks, and play clothes go in the dresser; school and dressy clothes go in the closet. Place socks, underwear, and undershirts in smaller containers (such as shoeboxes) inside the drawer for control. This way, even if the child rummages through a container looking for that certain pair of socks, it's only the sock container that's a shambles and not the entire drawer. Fold play outfits together (as we described for two-piece items in the baby's room chapter). Match up school outfits, too, hanging a coordinated shirt over a matching skirt or pair of pants. You can see how this system raises a child's standard of living. You've eliminated the chance that your child will look tacky and bedraggled.

School outfits will stay looking nicer longer (even if this is just jeans and sweatshirts) if the child changes into play clothes after school. (Play clothes are the patched or faded jeans, the sweatsuits with the patched knee, or anything that's lost that "just bought" sparkle yet has plenty of wear left.)

Everywhere we go, people ask what to do with their mountains of hand-me-downs. Here are our three rules:

1. Keep only quality. Don't store play clothes because the child is constantly in the process of creating new ones. Look for these telltale signs: a worn seat, underarms, or elbows, and stains; lost shape, especially in knits; and faded fabric.

2. **Mend keepers before storing.** This lessens the chance that they'll become dead storage and increases the chance that they'll be worn. If you honestly have no intention of mending them, pass them on to charity.

3. **Store efficiently.** You can label one end of a box so the contents can be noted at a glance. But if you have a variety of contents and a quantity of boxes, we suggest you take author Daryl Hoole's advice. She recommends storing things in numbered boxes and keeping a 3 x 5-inch card on every box of stored items, with the number of the card matched to the number of a box. (The family home computer can also be the spot to list this information.) Itemize box contents on the card and indicate the storage location. Again, this will increase the chances of these items being worn. Store only what can be used, then use what you store.

Living the Law of Household Ecology (when something new comes in, something else must go out) is one of the best ways to keep control of the number of clothes you manage. When you add new clothes, get rid of some old clothes. Sounds almost wasteful—after all, won't you need those clothes someday? Probably not—but you will always need your space.

Keep an ever-filling charity bag or box in your laundry area. Clothes are always wearing out, being grown out of, and going out of style. Don't give clothes a lifetime parking place in any dresser or closet.

DRESSER

When the blow dryer, curling iron, hot rollers, crimper, or straightening wand are used in the bedroom, they're often found tangled amongst each other on the dresser top. Here again, since we're discussing real life, we recognize your teenage daughter may seldom take the time to separate each appliance, wrap and secure each cord, then neatly tuck them away into an assigned center. But set up a hair appliance center anyway (they can be hung, boxed, or bagged), then the reasonable responsibility for the order of these items rests fully with her. (At least she can no longer say, "I don't have anyplace to put them!")

Keep the dresser top clear. Children can probably handle a lamp, a framed photo, or both. But remember, you're trying to create a room your children can maintain. Make it easy for them.

TOYS, BOOKS, GAMES, SPORTS EQUIPMENT

Streamline to weed out all the broken toys; tired stuffed animals; books with broken backs, lost covers, and ripped pages; and games with broken or missing pieces. Check the interest rating on these things, too. If they no longer hold interest, get rid of them.

Toys will pay for themselves and earn their keep if they are high-quality and open-ended or "doing" toys (such as building blocks, dolls, play tea sets, Lincoln Logs, interlocking plastic blocks, G.I. Joes, and so on). Toys that draw on the imagination are a child's friend for years.

Group toys into small drawstring bags or containers with lids. These full drawstring bags can be hung on an inside closet wall or from a wall-mounted pegboard equipped with pegboard hooks. Alice's children use large pegboards cut in shapes and decorated to match their room decors. For instance, her boys' room is trimmed in an old-fashioned paneled truck stenciling, so their pegboard is cut in the same paneled truck shape and painted to match. Her daughters' pegboard is cut in the shape of a house. (See illustrations.) Each shape is approximately four feet high and five feet long.

Be sure to rotate toys from time to time, putting some up out of sight. Keep a selection tucked away to bring out whenever a babysitter comes, too—this eases a potentially tense situation. Doll collections can sit on a child's bed, in a cradle or buggy, in a child's rocker, or on a low shelf. Some types of dolls, such as the ever-popular Barbie dolls, can be kept in drawstring bags, with their clothing and accessories.

A truck-shaped pegboard is an attractive decoration as well as a useful holder for drawstring bags.

The pegboards in Alice's children's rooms are part of the decor—a truck for the boys and a house for the girls.

Books are a child's window on the world; they become warm friends forever. Make good books a part of your home. Preserve preschool and some choice children's books by folding strips of clear, wide library tape over the bottom edge of each page to keep edges from tearing. (This tape can be purchased at most office supply stores.) Three-inch-wide strips of clear contact paper can serve the same purpose. Special treasures such as scouting handbooks will last longer and become permanent records of advancement if you cover the jackets completely with clear contact paper.

Don't give space to games no one likes, or games with broken or missing pieces. Keep only family favorites. Get the keepers out of their rickety cardboard boxes. (We're convinced cardboard game boxes do more than their share to undermine the mental health of the American home manager.) Keep the instructions, though, and follow home efficiency expert and author Daryl Hoole's advice: Glue the instructions onto the backs of their respective game boards. (Consider keeping a photocopy of these rules with the game parts to refer to, should there be questions during the game.) Group all like game parts together into little labeled containers, placing tokens in one container, marbles in another, dice in another, and so on. Store these small containers in one large master container.

If there's no room in your children's rooms for their personal sports equipment, then try to centralize it. Group it together in like categories and store it in one central location. We use a heavy drawstring bag for all balls, bats, and mitts. These bags give order and control to practically any category of sports equipment. And they can be hung from studs along garage or storage area walls. Bagging things up isn't a guarantee that there will be no more roller skates or baseball bats lying in the middle of the front walk or on the basement stairs, but it's a help. And the system will at least free a child's closet and bedroom space of some clutter.

Have more space and control of boardgames by removing them from their cardboard boxes and storing the small parts in a master container.

For making drawstring bags, consider saving some "tosser" men's pants. Cut the legs off at the crotch and discard them. Turn the cutoffs inside out, sew straight across the bottom, and you have created an instant bag. Turn right side out and run your drawstring through the belt loops. (For more help with drawstring bag ideas, see Back-of-the-Book Bonuses.)

WALLS

Like the master bedroom, a child's or teen's room is not finished until you deal with the walls. Keep them simple, set standards, and exert some control over what will and will not be displayed in your children's rooms. See to it that your child's immediate world—his or her room—is a positive world. You might be able to talk your poster-loving child into rotating a few, as you do the toys, for a fresh and uncluttered look. Traditional wall items include a framed mirror, bulletin board, college or sports pennants, framed photos of the child and family, framed art prints, stenciling, and wall graphics.

Speaking of wall graphics, here is a resourceful idea to not only decorate expansive wall areas, but to designate individual display areas and visually divide space in the shared room situation. If possible, assign sides of the room to each child. Then, using acrylic paints and masking tape as your outline and guide, paint each child's name on his or her respective wall in large block letters. Make your letters approximately two feet tall by one foot wide and place each name on its side, running it vertically up the wall, starting at the floor and

In this corner of a kid's room, college pennants hang at ceiling level to add interest as well as visual space. Posters hang as a grouping, occupying floor to ceiling space, and a minimum is kept on the dresser top.

proceeding up to the ceiling, or vice versa. There are dozens of different design options for this kind of graphic. Choose one that suits both you and the children.

Take time to teach the older children the same basic design principles that will be discussed in the next chapter on living rooms; talk about balance and scale of objects in relation to the wall, placement of objects on the wall, and so on.

There are many sources of bedroom overload, and one of the hardest to deal with is extended family and well-meaning friends. One favor you could do your children, as well as yourself, is to give your relatives and friends some suggestions for meaningful, long-lasting gifts. Examples for the older child to teenager might include:

- Sports and college pennants
- Hair salon gift certificates
- Hope chest items, or a hope chest
- Special bedding, such as hand-tied or quilted comforters
- "Time-with-you" coupons
- Good books
- Clip-on headboard reading light
- Purse or billfold with tickets to a sporting event tucked inside
- Telephone accompanied by the *Toll-free Digest* (over seventeen thousand listings for free, informative calls)
- Gift certificate from the telephone company
- Gift certificate from a favorite clothing store
- Gift certificate from a local theatre, tickets for two
- Registration for a craft class at the local sewing or specialty shop
- Gift certificates from the local pizza parlor
- Savings bonds or a mutual fund established under the Uniform Gift to Minors Act
- An attractive container holding glue, scissors, cellophane tape, thumbtacks, staples and stapler, and so on
- Anything pertaining to a specific hobby they might be involved in
- Origami book and paper (the art of paper folding)
- Monogrammed bath sheet
- Kaleidoscope
- Electric pencil sharpener
- Subscription to a favorite magazine

And for the smaller child:

- Small change purse containing not only change, but a book of passes to an ice cream or frozen yogurt parlor, hamburger chain, miniature golf, ice skating, and so on
- Copies of classic children's stories such as *Winnie the Pooh, Charlotte's Web, The Reluctant Dragon, Where the Wild Things Are, Peter Rabbit, The Velveteen Rabbit, The Little Engine that Could,* and so on
- Cassette story tapes with accompanying storybooks
- Birthstone jewelry
- Teddy bear
- Swimming lessons
- Step stool with the child's name painted on it

- Portrait gift certificate
- Slumber bag
- Bulletin board
- Memory box
- Tooth-fairy pillow
- School backpack
- Ready-made cowboy, Indian, fairy or princess, animal, or military costumes
- Puppets
- Miniature farm or Fort Apache play sets
- Watercolor paint box and sketchpad
- Magnifying glass
- Flashlight
- One- or two-man dome tent
- Scouting equipment, such as a mess kit, canteen, Pinewood Derby car kit, and so on

MAKING THE IMPROVEMENT LAST

Keeping the room streamlined means you will need to thoroughly orient your children as to what goes where and why it goes there. You'll also need to be consistent with the morning room inspection. This is the one action that will tell children you're serious about this change. From now on there will be no more overload mismanagement. This kid-ready room will be a constant source of opportunities for a reasonable amount of responsibility, and you'll see consistent, positive results.

EIGHT

FROM "NO-PLACE" TO "SHOW-PLACE"

Spiffing up the world's window on you — the living room

A living room isn't as purely functional as a bath or kitchen; nor is it as personal as a bedroom. Yet it's a key room in almost every home – the room visitors see first, sometimes the only room they spend time in. For that reason, many home managers take greater pains with this room than with any other room in the house to make it look just right. In fact, our surveys tell us this is the number one, most favored room in the home. The reason our respondents give? It's the prettiest and stays the neatest the longest.

When it comes to streamlining, you may find there is not as much obvious clutter here as elsewhere, precisely because the living room is so public a space. This isn't always the case, though; some living rooms are the center of their home's traffic patterns, and look it, with all the scattered possessions that go with a central location. Sometimes living room clutter is more subtle – a classic case of surface neatness, or decorative items that don't represent your family's values, tastes, and interests. Whichever type of overload you're seeing in your living room, the cure should be a familiar one to you by now.

Before you start the actual streamlining process, determine the specific purpose or purposes of *your* living room. That's not as obvious as it sounds, since this differs from home to home, depending on what other rooms are available, the age (and number) of family members, and the lifestyle that prevails at your house. If, for example, you have another room for TV watching, then you can reserve the living room for conversation, entertaining, reading, and similar pursuits. One thing your living room should not be is a kitchen annex. We've seen living rooms where people regularly ate and drank, at the visible expense of the furnishings and carpet. Save your furnishings (and your cleaning time) by limiting food consumption to the kitchen or dining room.

Once the purpose is assigned, hold to it. Family or recreation rooms are better for active pastimes, if you have such rooms. The living room, ideally, is the place for best behavior, good manners, decorum. If there are children in your home, the living room can serve as the laboratory for practicing their social graces.

CLEARING CLUTTER

Getting rid of living room overload starts with getting rid of outdated newspapers, magazines, and catalogs—even if you haven't read them yet. Sort through and tear out articles that you'll want to file; put these in the To File box. Make this routine a habit in the future to avoid repeat newspaper/magazine buildup. Don't try to take care of your To File box until your entire home is streamlined. You'll find that after every space in your house is simplified and under control, you'll not only have the physical but the mental energy to tackle what can be a most overwhelming chore—the files. In fact, for many chronic clippers who are paralyzed at the thought of tackling this job, we sometimes advise junking past collections and starting afresh. In any case, files probably need at least quarterly streamlining. Go through them and ask yourself the same key questions you asked on all the other things in your home, watching especially for obsolescence of information.

The living room piano is a classic site of potential clutter. Sheet music and music books are usually the biggest problem. If you have the very practical type of piano bench with a seat that opens up for storage, be sure to efficiently use that space. Or put the most frequently used materials atop or beside the piano in a book-sized wicker or rattan basket or other attractive container with handles. When practice is over, the books are easy to put away in their assigned spot; when they're needed for lessons, it's easy to carry along the entire container. Separate music into different categories, according to grade level or type. Consider putting music that is rarely used somewhere removed from the piano—for example, on a shelf in a bookcase or built-in storage unit. If you have a lot of music stored this way, you might want to set up a filing system so you can find specific pieces easily.

Besides being smothered by piles of music, the piano top also has a tendency to collect family photographs, stacks of mail, knickknacks, children's school papers, and the ubiquitous trailing philodendron. To clear the surface, mount the photos attractively on the wall, assign another drop-off spot for mail and school papers, and ruthlessly evaluate the knickknacks to eliminate some. If there's no better place for the philodendron, try winding it back through itself for a more compact, fuller plant. Clearing the piano top will create a fresh appearance as well as make for easier dusting.

Evaluate other surfaces, such as coffee, sofa, and end tables, fireplace mantels, hearths, and windowsills. Knickknack and accessory overload can easily get the best of these spots. Collect things that have special meaning to you, because you will be sacrificing space to hold them, and time and energy to care for them. Avoid overloading these tempting areas with too many sentimental or trendy knickknacks. There is a place in our homes and lives for the sentimental, but not at the expense of function, order, and good taste. Be sure your accessories are saying what you want them to about you.

For example, a woman who attended one of our seminars asked us what to do with the many antique porcelain dolls that were resting all over her living room. In talking with her, we could tell they meant a great deal to her and she really didn't want to part with them. The solution: Get rid of every bit of clutter so that these treasures can be seen and receive the attention they deserve. Then group them together, perhaps in pretty oak-splint baskets, onto child-sized antique chairs, or into beautiful wooden or wicker doll cradles. We've heard of other collectors who keep their doll collections in glass-fronted (and -topped) cases—this saves a lot of dusting. This approach will work with many collections—group or cluster them together for drama and focus, rather than sprinkling them throughout the room.

The key is to make sure that what you want to be noticed *is* noticed. Your special decorator touches can't compete with clutter. Clutter creates a visual distraction that robs a room of the chance to look its best, even if your accessories are of the finest quality and highest price. So give your decorator touches the opportunity to do what they were meant to do in the first place—be seen—by removing their visual competition—clutter.

UNCONDITIONAL SURRENDER

Get rid of all living room furnishings and accessories that have broken parts or are tattered and torn beyond repair. Constantly using, maintaining, and looking at shabby or shoddy items is depressing. One attractive lamp is much better than two or three that desperately need junking. As radical as it may sound, we advocate going without until you can have something of quality. After all, possessions are a subtle reflection of our attitudes, self-image, and even self-respect.

Consider, too, the quantity of furnishings in relation to the size of the room. Is there too much stuff? If so, can some pieces be put to better use in other rooms? Here's another reason to evaluate motives. Are you trying to impress someone? Are *things* giving you your identity? Are the people living in your home as precious to you as all the stuff you're collecting? Are visitors picking up the right message about how you feel about self, family, values, interests, and so forth? Even if your furniture is in good shape and beautiful, too much of a good thing is overwhelming and visually confusing. Remove some of the pieces and see if the effect isn't calmer and more peaceful.

WALLS

Living room walls are often magnets for clutter, too. Because walls have so much visual impact in a room, they are definitely decorating statements, whether you've made them consciously or unconsciously. Think about it. Are visitors getting the impression you own stock in the local antique or bric-a-brac stores? Are you filling your walls with trendy or faddish decor only because you don't know what else to put there? There's nothing wrong with these decorating ideas, *if* you really like them, *if* you don't overdo them, and *if* they are meaningful to you. Even if it means you have some bare spots on your walls, you'll find greater satisfaction if what is hung reflects your individuality, values, and family personality.

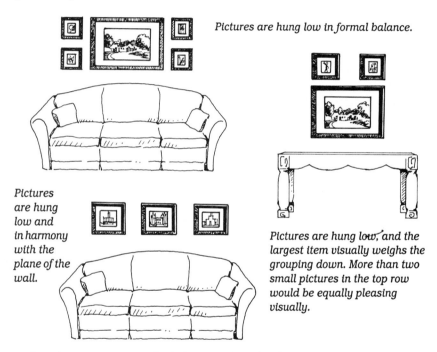

Pictures are hung low in formal balance.

Pictures are hung low and in harmony with the plane of the wall.

Pictures are hung low, and the largest item visually weighs the grouping down. More than two small pictures in the top row would be equally pleasing visually.

Pay close attention to the balance and scale of the things you hang. Don't hang a tiny object all alone on a large wall; it will get lost and lose its effectiveness. Group it with other items for greater impact. Don't hang a huge piece on a small wall, either. It's a good idea to visually divide your wall into vertical thirds and place objects along one of these invisible dividing lines. Avoid the tendency to place things in the exact center of any wall, as this approach is unimaginative and bland, and causes the object being hung to compete with the equal portions of space on either side of it. The empty space on either of the "thirds" sides will balance the objects hung on the other side. When you hang things, try to keep a single dominant item, or the focal point of a group, at or below eye level.

Avoid the tendency to hang anything on service walls. Service walls are those little slivers of wall that are found between doorjambs and corners, or between doorjambs and other doorjambs or window frames. These four- to six-inch pieces of wall are meant for holding up door and window frames, not for decorating. Using these areas as backgrounds for hanging objects tends to clutter and overload a room visually and make it feel smaller than it truly is.

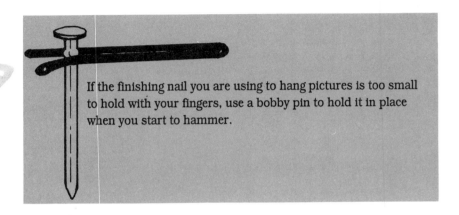

If the finishing nail you are using to hang pictures is too small to hold with your fingers, use a bobby pin to hold it in place when you start to hammer.

One last don't for walls: Do not hang pictures on the diagonal. Doing this fights the natural horizontal or vertical plane of the wall. People do this to fill space when they have a minimum amount of wall decor to work with. But, contrary to popular opinion, hanging on the diagonal does not fill extra space, and it looks dated and tacky. The only exception to hanging pictures diagonally is down a stairway wall. Here you have a natural diagonal plane to follow, and it works well.

DECORATIVE DEVICES

True, we've just warned you about decorating for the sake of decorating. But here are some ideas you may not have come across that you might want to adapt to your own use.

- If you are fortunate enough to have a front entry hall, hanging a nicely framed or pleasingly shaped mirror on one of its walls is a charming and practical touch. A mirror placed here will be convenient for both you and your guests—a good place for you to check your "face value" before entering a room full of people.

Stenciling can be applied around a living room window or door.

- Plants enhance any room if they're healthy and properly positioned. They're especially useful for adding a lived-in and furnished look to a sparsely furnished living room. For greater impact, and to avoid having "lived-in" turn to "cluttered," group plants together rather than scattering them one to a section. And, of course, display only well-maintained plants in clean, attractive containers. If you hate discarding a plant that's starting to look tired, move it to a less public room and try to nurse it back to health. We also suggest you avoid hanging your plants. However pretty your macrame hanger might be, hanging plants around a room adds to the visual clutter, especially if you have quite a bit going on with your walls.
- Stenciling is a classical, inexpensive, attractive, and personal approach to decorating. (We've listed a helpful and appealing book on the subject under "Suggested Reading" at the end of this book.) Consider stenciling borders along the top of your walls to substitute for built-in moldings; you can create a similar effect at chair-rail level or a dress-up effect around simply treated windows.
- Another idea is to create a meaningful display of family heritage and an-

cestry items. Pauline's family room wall, for example, holds a few iron tools that her father-in-law and grandfather-in-law used for years on their family farm. Alice's dining area wall holds a porcelain alphabet bowl-type dinner dish that her father-in-law used for meals when he was a small child. The same wall holds a quilted hanging made from an antique General Mills flour sack, with logo and printing intact. Her mother and grandmother saved these cloth sacks, tried to bleach them white, and made them over into slips, panties, pantaloons, and dish towels. Displaying your family crest or some handiwork from your ancestors' native land (or lands) is an effective way to establish a sense of family legacy. It's also a refreshing change and can do a lot to make your home uniquely yours.

Items handed down from past generations form a unique and personal wall grouping.

PROBLEM SOLVING

Not all living rooms are fully furnished, beautifully proportioned, or used just for quiet adult activities. If you live in a rental unit, you may not even be able to experiment much, if at all, with stenciling or other paint treatments or with wall hangings without risking financial penalties. But no matter what your dwelling, you *can* make your living room a place you're proud to welcome guests to. Remember, it's not what you have, but what you do with what you have that counts.

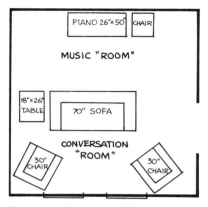

Centered sofa, room-within-a-room.

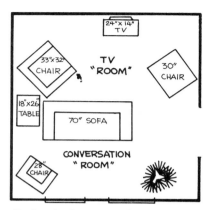

Back-to-back, room-within-a-room.

Living room 13' x 13'9"

Minimum of furniture; plants fill in spaces.

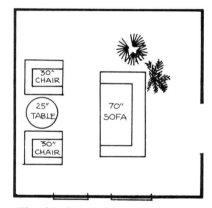

'Shrinking" space by arranging a room around an imaginary wall.

If the movement of furniture is scratching your beautiful floors, put self-sticking bunion pads on the bottoms of furniture feet and legs.

So experiment until you like what you have. You might, for example, group your furniture in arrangements to give the appearance of a room-within-a-room — especially effective if you have only a few pieces to fill up a generous-sized space. Try placing a large piece, such as a sofa, in the approximate center of the room. Or use a back-to-back grouping. A combination of both techniques also works well to achieve a room-within-a-room look. The basic idea is to stop lining the walls with furniture and avoid squeezing things into the corners of the room. You might also try to create new "walls" in your imagination, and place all or the majority of your living room furniture in one part of the room.

Another budget-wise technique you can use to "furnish" a streamlined, sparsely furnished room is to place your wall decor low. This treatment visually takes the place of furniture and makes a room feel full because you are filling in spaces that the eye is attracted to first, the walls. Because attention naturally gravitates toward walls, the room will look and feel more completely furnished if the walls are done well.

Pictures placed low on a wall fill space when furniture is sparse.

DREAMS INTO REALITY

Unhappy with the looks of this or any other room in the home? Then try the Projects and Dreams Worksheet on page 80 and 81 for transforming vague wants and wishes into concrete reality.

For instance, perhaps your living room windows need updating. You decide on microblinds (the "What" blank). This will take some saving for (the "Starting Date" blank). "Target Completion Date" refers to the point in time when the money has been accumulated, and the blinds are purchased and installed. You note the date you'll have the money, the date you'll place your order, when the blinds will be picked up or delivered, and when they'll be installed. All this is logged into the "Agenda" section. The "Resources" portion of the page is to aid in the cross-shopping you'll do to make sure you get the best buy. The last section, "Expenses," is to do the obvious—keep you within your budget.

> When shopping for furniture, consider other sources besides local furniture stores and department store furniture departments: yard sales, auctions, secondhand shops, office supply stores (many of these furnishings blend durability with sleek, contemporary styling), catalogs, unfinished furniture outlets, and discount stores (which sell ready-to-assemble furnishings that don't cost a fortune).

What if your dream is more complex and costly than simply changing window treatments? Henry L. Gantt, an early management consultant, explained that any in-depth project is made up of a number of interlocking projects (smaller plans) that are dependant upon each other and must be molded together under a time limitation. He designed a bar chart showing the relationship of time to various subprojects in a master plan. Assume you want to remodel your kitchen, knock out the wall that separates it from the garage, and convert the adjoining garage into a family room. You will be doing much of the work yourself in the evenings, after work, and you have approximately twelve weeks to accomplish this major project—the warm summer months of June, July, and August. You will also need to continue living in the house and using the kitchen most of the time. You might construct a Gantt-type chart (see pages 82 and 83) to break the project down into do-able subprojects over the twelve-week period.

The Gantt chart has been used for years by industry and business, even the armed forces, to accomplish huge undertakings. It's a commonsense idea that can be applied to something as simple as putting in your next vegetable or flower garden. This excellent approach to turning wants and wishes into reality keeps

PROJECTS AND DREAMS WORKSHEET

What: *Micro blinds for living room (2 sets) $190.00 budget*

Starting Date: *April 1*   Target Completion Date: *August 31*

Agenda:
money acquired: July 15
order date: July 16
pick-up date: August 30
installation date: August 31

RESOURCES

Who:	What:	Where:	Phone:
Sears	*174.39 (sale)*	*mall*	*735-0001*
Penney's	*169.79 (cat.)*	*mall*	*783-9422*
Costco	*171.98*	*Harris Blvd.*	*783-8888*
Drapery Mart	*185.95*	*Denton*	*547-0101*

EXPENSES

What: *2 sets*   Amount: *169.79*
micro 1/2" blinds   *tax*   *13.60*
                          $183.39

PROJECTS AND DREAMS WORKSHEET

What: _____

_____

Starting Date: _____ Target Completion Date:_____

Agenda: _____

_____

_____

_____

_____

_____

_____

_____

RESOURCES

Who:	What:	Where:	Phone:
_____	_____	_____	_____
_____	_____	_____	_____
_____	_____	_____	_____
_____	_____	_____	_____
_____	_____	_____	_____

EXPENSES

What: _____ Amount: _____

_____

_____

_____

_____

_____

GANTT BAR CHART

STARTING DATE:												
WHAT: Kitchen/Garage Remodeling	Time Measured in Weeks											
Subprojects	1	2	3	4	5	6	7	8	9	10	11	12
Prepare master plan; price materials; obtain bids.	▓											
Streamline garage; relocate keeper contents (yard and garden equipment, minimal auto maintenance tools) to shed by the garden.		▓										
Knock out kitchen wall adjoining garage; remove garage window, front garage door, back garage door, kitchen window.			▓	▓								
Frame in garage door areas, new family room window areas, and new kitchen garden window area.					▓							
Frame in drop ceiling for kitchen recessed lighting, new kitchen back door.						▓						
Remove existing kitchen cupboards, countertops, flooring, old appliances.							▓					
Rewire family room and kitchen, install new receptacles.								▓				
Install insulation and sheet rock.									▓			
Install kitchen recessed lighting panels, family room lighting system.									▓			
Install new cupboards, countertops, plumbing, appliances.										▓		
Paint and wallpaper both rooms; install vinyl and carpet; hang wall decor, move in furniture.											▓	

GANTT BAR CHART

STARTING DATE:												
What:	Time Measured in Weeks											
Subprojects	1	2	3	4	5	6	7	8	9	10	11	12

the stress and inconvenience to a minimum, and keeps you within your money and time budget.

Speaking of budgets, "There's no money for anything new" is not an honest or valid excuse for not upgrading the rooms in your home. What you are really saying is, "I don't want to spend money on that now." This is America, the home of the free and the land of plenty. And there *is* money for most anything you may want to purchase or do to a room. You just have to "find" it. Over the years we have "found" money for our wants and wishes by taking on a paper route, selling off our clutter and overload, recycling newspapers and aluminum cans, and holding back a few dollars here and there from our grocery money. Pauline has sold fruit-bearing starts from her raspberry patch for a dollar a dozen to "find" the money for a watch that her son desperately wanted. Alice and her high-school-aged daughter made and sold apple pies for five dollars apiece to help fund a school trip to Washington, D.C. This is still the land of opportunity, and we know firsthand that if you want something badly enough, you can find a way to get it.

Consistently upgrading and beautifying our rooms (as opposed to maintaining status quo) is one of the more subtle facets to home management. The human spirit needs to see visual evidence that things are continually improving and progressing. "Gazing on beautiful things," Michelangelo once wrote, "acts on my soul, which thirsts for heavenly light." What was true for Michelangelo is also true for us today. So don't waste time whining about how crummy things might look or complaining about what you don't have. Get rid of what you don't like, use, need, want, or have room for, develop to the maximum what you do have, and use the Projects and Dreams Worksheet to help you obtain those items you want and need.

NINE

ALL IN THE FAMILY

The comfortable life where you *really* live:
the family room

S omewhere in your house, there's probably a room where everyone congre-
gates; you may call it the den, or the family room, or the rec room, but
whatever its name, it serves the same purpose. If you're fortunate enough
to have such a room, you've probably noticed that it has a tendency to be a
"nobody cares" room. "Don't eat that popcorn in the living room—take it to the
family room," or "You can play with your toys in the family room," or "If you're
going to wrestle, do it in the family room" are common instructions in many
households. This room, by any name, is a carefree, casual place because it's
often out of sight of the living room, and therefore of the outside world. It gets
messy, cluttered, even abused. All the same, there's much more to it than that.
In fact, a nicer way to think of this all-purpose place is the "make-yourself-at-
home" room.

If you're going to have a place that's comfortable but also well maintained
and uncluttered, you'll need to take a good look around the family room and
determine where comfort ends and shabbiness or carelessness begins. Take a
look at the worn-out sofa, worn-through or stained carpet, broken-backed
books, drooping draperies, flat cushions, and so on. Then think how carefully
you've decorated your living room, putting your best effort out front. Don't
subject yourself and your family—who deserve the best—to leftovers. Don't
relegate unfixables, or things you've never liked in the first place, to the family
room; don't be afraid to discard items that aren't good enough. Turn this room
into one that can be carefree, but never care-less.

Start by deciding on a purpose or purposes for the room. It may be the place
in your home with the most diverse assignments, so carefully define each area
of the room and insist that these decisions be honored. This is an excellent
place to use a room-within-a-room furniture arrangement. (See Chapter 8.) You
can direct your attention into specific areas by creating centers inside this single
family room space.

For example, if your family room houses a television, group comfortable
seating around it, leaving space for other activities in the remainder of the room.

An activity center is created when all boardgames and puzzles are stored together. If space for this center is limited, try eliminating the cardboard boxes and using a master container for all game and puzzle parts. (See Chapter 7.)

This is also the place for your VCR, Nintendo equipment, and video collection. What you have now created is a family media center. If there's room, you may even want to include your compact disc recorder and CDs, or your stereo and cassettes. We see many people accumulating this equipment before they get the actual furniture — the entertainment center — that it goes into. Thus, the clutter and constant eyesore of snaking tangled cords, piles of game cartridges scattered all over, and stacks of videos atop the VCR or TV drives them nuts.

So what's to be done until this wonderful piece of furniture can be purchased? We suggest you deal with this area as you did the piano and its assorted clutter (living room chapter). Make sure all videos, cassettes, game cartridges, and CDs are either in their original cases and covers, or are labeled appropriately. Then separate these items into adequately sized and handsome containers. Square and rectangular wicker baskets are one suggestion. Remember to evaluate, using our key questions (do you still like this tape, do you still want it, do you still use it, do you still need it, do you still have room for it in your collection), as you assign your accumulation to your various containers. Then comes the challenge of finding the best spot for this stuff. If there's a bookcase

Encourage hobbyists to work in a family room hobby center by storing all supplies there.

in this room, you may be able to make space for video cassettes, perhaps even Nintendo cartridges, on a shelf, after some thorough book streamlining. Much of this paraphernalia, however, will probably sit on the floor near the TV or music equipment—thus the reason for handsome containers—they just might need to look like and serve as decorative touches.

If the negative influences of television concern you, look for ways to play down its attraction as much as possible. A dark empty screen begs to be turned on, so try turning it around, put it in a closet when it's not in use, shut the entertainment center doors on it, or (here's our best and boldest suggestion) get rid of it.

You'll find the remainder of the space in the family room has lots of possibilities. Consider creating a hobby or game center with a table and chairs (small ones for the children). Or use floor cushions or beanbag chairs grouped around bookshelves to create a reading corner; place an area rug close to toy containers to make an inviting play center. If your family room includes a Ping-Pong or pool table, then keep everything that relates to it in one area, all related pieces in one container, and resist the tendency to use these flat surfaces as unofficial drop-off spots. More and more family rooms today are the location for the computer center, also. This can mean another space challenge, what with all the accompanying extras and furniture needs. But you get the idea. No matter *how* your family members spend their time, you can develop attractive centers that will catch their attention and make them welcome in this special area or room of your home.

GETTING RID OF BOOKS: IT'S A DIRTY JOB, BUT SOMEBODY HAS TO DO IT

Your family room may double as a family library. And that's great—books have a magic about them and are a wonderful part of any life and any home. But that very magic sometimes makes it hard to get rid of any. Since even books carry with them a space and maintenance price, they, like other items, must be dealt with realistically. Here's how to keep them under control.

Get rid of broken or ripped books, or those with the covers torn off. Be especially tough on out-of-date textbooks. If you haven't used them in years, you aren't likely to use them at all. If you can find the same or more current material at the library, you'll need a tremendously convincing reason to justify keeping those old space-robbing texts.

Save some in boxes, if absolutely necessary. If, after simplifying the book collection, you still have a book or stack of books that for one reason or another can't be parted with but don't merit shelf space, box them up. An example of this type of book might be childhood copies of nursery rhymes, fairy tales, fables, and so on, that family members have outgrown but want to save to pass on to future generations. To this day we're envious of our friends who had the foresight to save original copies of their grade school primers—the *Dick and Jane* series. What treasures—and what a pleasure it would be to share them with our children now. The word "treasure" brings up a point. Treasured books should be stored properly, taking into consideration climate and packaging. *If* you have space, we recommend they be kept on your bookshelves. Store them only if you cannot devote shelf space to them, in which case you should list the titles on a 3x5-inch card, make a note where the box is stored, and number-code the box and the card. This card will go in your file and the box will go to a remote corner in the garage, basement, attic, or other storage area, where you can forget about it. They will be safe, accessible, and most important, out of the way.

Arrange the remaining keepers attractively. Group books together according to subject matter rather than size.

Perhaps you've noticed that this is the area in your home that can accommodate ultrapersonal decorating touches. Here is where your son's framed stamp or butterfly collection can hang. Here is a wonderful place to hang an antique quilt, or to set up a new quilt top that's in need of quilting. Your spinning wheel or loom plus a basket of handspun yarn can sit here. Your vast assortment of family photos always displays well in this room. Even though any of this would be fine in the living room, the implied coziness of the family room seems to suit it better.

Making some adjustments in the room you REALLY live in will turn an area that often looks as though nobody cares into a cozy, inviting, and in-control "make-yourself-at-home" room.

TEN

MAKING YOUR KITCHEN MEASURE UP

Creating convenient centers for people and activities

N ow for the big one. The room you can't wait to streamline, yet dread starting on. This is one of the busiest spots in the house. It's your family's private fast-food center, dining hall, gathering place—a food and people station. It's been called the hub of the home because it's a multipurpose area with many demands placed upon it. Even the list that follows may not present the whole story. A kitchen is a:

- ✔ Storage depot for food, utensils, and equipment
- ✔ Key work center for food preparation and cleanup
- ✔ Area of the home where food is most often eaten
- ✔ Social center
- ✔ Information center
- ✔ Office center
- ✔ Place to do homework
- ✔ Hobby center
- ✔ Small-scale cannery

Over two-thousand questionnaire respondents have told us the kitchen is the next least favorite room in the home (after the bathroom) because it's such a busy place, always being undone; it never stays clean and orderly for long. Working in an overloaded, out-of-control kitchen is self-defeating; maintaining it is time-, energy-, and spirit-consuming. You've probably noticed that it is not only stressful to you, but can also be difficult for others to deal with. That's why the kitchen needs to be streamlined down to the bare bones: People + kitchen activies + overload = Mess, confusion, and lack of control. Eliminating the overload reduces the mess factor, removes much of the confusion, and increases the control people have over this area. So, for a kitchen that "measures up" to the demands placed on it, give it a thorough streamlining.

Streamlining the overloaded kitchen means dealing with more than drawers and cupboards. It means getting everything off the countertops and keeping these things inside their respective centers. It means a bare minimum (ideally nothing) on the work area walls, that is, the walls above and surrounding all counters and large appliances. Kitchens and their contents accumulate greasy dust and fly specks; they are visually busy because the walls are cut up by cupboards, windows, appliances, and entry ways. Hanging anything on these walls creates more work because hung items need frequent washing; what's more, even the cleanest collection can look cluttered at the tilt of a mug.

Streamlining the kitchen also involves removing everything from the windowsill and refrigerator top—and keeping these spots clear. If there are open soffits, clear everything off them, too. We also suggest you clear off your refrigerator door as much as possible for easier cleaning. Your office and information centers might be better places for much of this material. Children's artwork, field trip permission slips, graded school papers, and so on can be displayed on your laundry or sewing area wall, the inside of an unpainted cupboard door, the outside or inside of a closet door, on the end of a bank of unpainted cupboards, or on a specially designated corkboard hung in the kitchen. One family we know purchased cork by the yard (enough to run floor to ceiling) at the local hardware store, and stapled it to the wall next to their kitchen back door. With the addition of mitered floor molding nailed all around, it is an attractively framed bulletin board with ample space for posting everyone's artwork, messages, lists, and so on.

GETTING STARTED

Webster's dictionary says a center is a place or point at which a specific activity is concentrated. This is exactly what a kitchen center is: Cleanup takes place at the cleanup center, or the sink area; cooking happens at the cooking center, or the stove area, and so forth. To get started, look closely at your living patterns. Assess what happens in your kitchen, then decide what you want to happen there. Plan centers around the latter, not the former.

Step 1 is to write these centers down and post them somewhere for quick reference. You don't have to decide where these centers *are* yet, just make a note of their names. (You will be assigning center sites in step 4.) These choices will be your guide, however, for how you organize what's left after streamlining.

The ideal kitchen, though not necessarily yours, might have a tableware center, cooking center, baking center, cleanup center, pantry area, and microwave center; these are the basics. If anyone packs a lunch or if there are older children who work in the kitchen, a sandwich or lunch center might be in order. Most kitchens have a phone, which means an information center is needed. If you use the kitchen table or a built-in desk for menu planning, bill paying, and checkbook balancing, then you will need a minioffice center. (This is also where incoming mail is handled daily. If you have indoor pets in the family and you feed them in the kitchen, then you may need a pet center. This area could house not only the pet food and pet snacks, but the pet shampoo, a container holding the grooming tools, and so on. Your kitchen may even need more centers – this depends on your lifestyle, available space, and what you want to happen in this room.

Several people we've worked with wanted a snack center. This amounted to a drawer or two for chips, crackers, pretzels, nuts, dried fruit, and so on. A farmhouse kitchen we streamlined needed a dairy center to accommodate the equipment and utensils used in the family milking business. One of our "patients," a gourmet cook, needed a convenient spot to set up as his "bon appetit" center. He needed space for his various cooking liqueurs, cold-pressed oils, exotic herbs and spices, his bouquet garni, white vanilla, garlic press, and so on. Two popular superspecialized centers are a beverage/liquor center and a popcorn center. You can see that kitchen centers have as much variety as the people who work in them.

With centers listed, it's time to begin the actual physical process of streamlining.

Step 2 involves emptying the entire kitchen – all drawers, cupboards, the pantry, countertops, refrigerator top, windowsills, tops of soffits, and even the broom closet. This is not the time to start pitching stuff (you'll do this in step 4); just *get it out* of the cupboards and so on. As you are emptying, place contents in logical groupings (dishes and table-related items in one pile, pots and pans in another, and so on). You may want to place these things in empty boxes, just to keep everything corralled. This is where it gets overwhelming – facing a never-ending sea of things and wondering where to put them all. Don't panic; there *will* be a proper place for every keeper. You will be filling garbage, charity, and Someplace Else bags or boxes to the brim. In fact, the average haul out of a typical kitchen is seven to ten full, thirty-gallon-sized trash bags. This means you'll have much less to put back and much more space to put it in. So keep going. This system works.

Step 3 is a little easier. Vacuum and wipe out all drawers and cupboards, the pantry, and so on. This is the time to add fresh shelf paper, if you use it.

Step 4 is to establish the location of all your centers, using your list. Begin with tableware, then cooking, then baking, then cleanup, then pantry, then microwave. Remember, though, nothing is sacred or set in stone. You may change your mind here and there and do some center juggling. That's OK. We have streamlined hundreds of kitchens, and every time we've changed our minds about some center locations. Fiddle around with it until you get it just right.

Now it's time to load your centers. But before you do, remember you are streamlining, and *not* reorganizing. So use our key questions on every single item in your kitchen and get rid of anything that's broken (that you know in the deep recesses of your mind you will *never* fix), anything that's worn out, or anything you no longer like, use, need, want, or have room for. Do this to food also. The most common offenders to look for in the food category are weevil and staleness. And if you're even close to typical, you'll probably find some very strange food items that you don't remember buying or can't remember *why* you bought—so toss them.

A word on kitchen tools, equipment, and appliances: All of us with family on the premises need and would appreciate more kitchen help. We have found that you can reasonably expect and get this help IF the kitchen is streamlined and IF the tools, equipment, and appliances they are supposed to use are clean and in good working order. For instance, *you* might have the patience and skill it takes to deftly wiggle and toggle the dishwasher knob to get the thing started— but do your kids? Even if they *do* know how, it's a bet they don't have the patience. You might know just how to stack all the pots and pans to get them into that tiny cupboard, but do your kids? And even if they *do* know how, it's a bet they seldom, if ever, do it right, because it's just too much of a hassle. So when you reload your cupboards and drawers with keepers, do it with an eye towards simplicity and efficiency. Part of this efficiency may mean having a few duplicate utensils, such as a couple rubber spatulas and wooden spoons (one of each for the baking and cooking centers). This will depend on available space. If you're tight on space, don't overload it with duplicates. Repair faulty appliances, update equipment, and replace broken tools, and you'll find yourself surrounded with fairly willing kitchen help.

The following guidelines will help you set up the basic centers, plus any others your lifestyle calls for.

TABLEWARE CENTER

This houses everything that is table related. For example:

- Dishes
- Glasses
- Pretty serving bowls (not plastic refrigerator keepers, microwave dishes, or mixing bowls—which will go someplace else)
- Flatware
- Table linens—placemats, tablecloths, napkins, napkin rings (*only* if you actually *use* these things, otherwise they don't deserve space)
- Candles and candleholders (same advice as above)
- Fancy serving pieces (Quit saving them for company; treat yourself and/ or your family special and USE nice things at your table, *every day.*)

- Salt and pepper shakers (attractive rather than the utilitarian style found at the stove)
- Attractive butter dish
- Table trivets
- Napkin holder
- Sugar bowl
- Jam or honey pot
- Syrup container

Add to or subtract from this list as it applies to you.

This center should be located closest to your table, not necessarily closest to your dishwasher. Place settings can sit in a cupboard, and flatware in a drawer. However, if there is no drawer available, place the tray of flatware on the cupboard shelf beside the place settings. Keep an open mind on this suggestion. While it may strike you as inconvenient at first, the extra drawer space it gives you may be worth it. It bears repeating: In this space-crunched world, not everything can be at fingertip reach—sometimes we must endure a little inconvenience for the sake of order and control.

Be selective as you fill this center. No more chipped, cracked, stained, or ugly dishes on your table. No more dingy, plastic, mismatched or commercial-type glasses at the table. Try to have only matching glassware at all place settings (this is a real morale booster). Set aside a number of your plastic or mismatched glasses (the number will vary according to the size of your family) for use as water glasses. These glasses take only a small space near the sink or refrigerator. Put them in a drawer, where they can be laid flat, or in a sliver of available cupboard space. All our clients have liked this water glass system because it keeps the table glasses free and clear for meals.

The salt and pepper shakers, sugar bowl, butter dish, syrup container, honey and jam pot, and so on go in the cupboard with your place settings. It is convenient to group them onto a small, round turntable, but if space doesn't permit this, then simply line them up along one wall of the tableware cupboard. If possible, place your candle holders (perhaps lying flat) and candles with your table linens. Can you see how much convenience is created by having all your table items grouped together? (Actually, there's nothing new under the sun. Restaurants have been using this system for hundreds of years.)

If you have young children capable of doing kitchen duty, consider putting dishes and glasses in the bottom cupboard closest to the table. This strategy alleviates the cupboard climbing and lessens chances for dish disasters. To keep baby/toddler fingers from destroying or being injured by the contents of cupboards and drawers, use childproof plastic locks (Kinder Locs), available in most hardware stores.

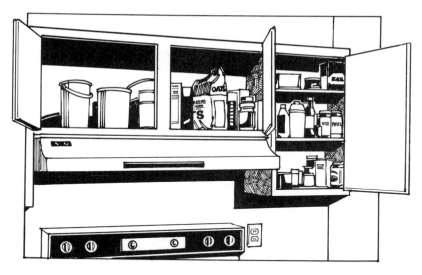

Cornstarch, cooked cereals, bouillons, sauce packets, hot drink mixes, herbs, and seasonings are stored in a cooking center's upper cupboard.

COOKING CENTER

This should be next to the stove and usually involves a couple of drawers, an upper cupboard, and a lower cupboard. The upper cupboard, most frequently located above the stove, holds:

- Salt and pepper shakers (This set, separate from the one in your table-ware center, will add convenience to your cooking routine.)
- All cooking herbs (There's a difference between what is used for baking and what is used for cooking; you don't bake a cake with sage and you don't cook up a white sauce with cinnamon.) Less frequently used herbs should not take up valuable kitchen space. Store these in your pantry or general food storage area. "Cooking center" herbs are those used several times a week. Note: If you're a cooking purist and are concerned about stove heat and fumes affecting the flavor of your herbs, then find another convenient spot for them. Just be sure they are as near the stove as possible. There are also special drawer inserts you can buy that allow you to store herbs in a nearby drawer.
- Cornstarch
- Gravy and sauce packets (nested neatly and conveniently in a container)
- Pastas
- Bouillon and hot-drink mixes
- Cooked cereals

- Small bottle of vegetable oil (Keep larger container in pantry and refill as necessary; this goes for all staples—small sizes in your centers and large sizes in your pantry.)
- Parmesan cheese
- Parsley flakes
- Chopped dried onions
- Boxed convenience dinner mixes (if there's room; otherwise, place them in the pantry center)

> To control spaghetti, unwrap it and put it in a spaghetti-sized drawstring bag (as opposed to the space-eating spaghetti *jars*), which you can make or purchase from a kitchen boutique. To conserve space, hang the bag on the inside of a cupboard door or on the inside cupboard wall.

If space is really tight, store less frequently used ingredients in the pantry or food storage area.

The drawers of this center, ideally one on each side of the stove, house nice pot holders and cooking utensils. Use drawer dividers to arrange the latter. The basic stove utensils are:

- Wire whisk
- Pair of tongs
- Rubber spatula
- Large spoon
- Metal turner
- Plastic turner
- Meat fork
- Two wooden spoons

In almost every instance, you only need one of each utensil. (The exception to this guideline was mentioned earlier: *if* you have plenty of space to accommodate duplicates.) This is a safe number—any more than one of each encourages overload. If you're convinced you need more than one of something, try washing the single utensil and reusing it. Work this way for twenty-one days and see if the extra space and order in your utensil drawer isn't worth the little inconvenience.

> Save time and tears by chopping onions in a blender. Section the onion, fill the blender with cold water, turn on the grate button for two or three seconds. Drain in colander. Spread chopped onion on cookie sheets and flash freeze. Then put in freezer bags and store in the freezer.

Almost every kitchen utensil can be hung. If you're really low on drawer space, then hang some of your utensils inside a cupboard wall or door of your cooking center, and group any nonhanging utensils in a container and set them in the potholder drawer. It is possible to put small finishing nails into very thin cupboard doors without puncturing the face of the door, if they are carefully hammered in at a severe angle. An alternative to pounding finishing nails is to use small plastic hooks backed with a strong adhesive; they're available in the housewares department of discount or department stores. Do *not* hang kitchen utensils on the wall above your stove or on another open wall, or they'll attract airborne grease and dust, which means a maintenance headache.

Be ruthless when deciding what to keep. In defense of chucking the broken, worn-out, rusty, chewed-up utensils, we've compiled a comparative price list for replacements. (All figures are approximate.)

Metal ladle	$2.19	Tongs	$1.69
Large slotted spoon	$1.69	Plastic spatula	$1.09
Rubber spatula	$1.29	Pancake turner	$1.69
Wooden spoons	3/$1.99	Large metal spoon	$1.69
Potato masher	$1.79	Large wire whisk	$2.29

Make a list of utensils that need replacing, and if it's not immediately possible to restock this entire drawer, replace one item at a time. Kitchen work can be more fun, even for the "I-hate-to-cook" folks, when there are nice tools and equipment to work with.

The lower cupboard of the cooking center holds:

- Pots
- Pans
- A few carefully chosen appliances such as the Crock-Pot, electric griddle, and frypan. Store detachable cords, wound and secured, with the appliance they go with. Either lay them inside these appliances, or hang them up along the inside of the cupboard door or wall.

Items in this center are used for cooking, not baking.

We consistently see kitchens loaded with too many pans and appliances. If you want more control and space in your kitchen, get rid of everything but the basics. Why give precious space to a hotdog cooker *and* a saucepan, when the saucepan will not only cook hotdogs, but hundreds of other things as well? Get rid of the hotdog cooker and all other single-purpose, space-eating appliances; keep only what's essential. A word should be said here about the new wave of under-the-cupboard, space-saving appliances on the market. While it's true that they *are* off the counter, it's also true that they are out in the open, susceptible to catching all the fly specks, greasy dust, and stray splatters of whipping cream or banana pudding that are a part of normal kitchen use. The hardware (screws, brackets, knobs, dials, cords, clamps, and so on) will also trap this gunk and create a maintenance nightmare. We're convinced this is a stupid way to save space—better to tuck your usual counter model appliances into a streamlined cupboard or drawer and save yourself not only space, but maintenance time as well.

Here are your basic pots, pans, and appliances for the cooking center:

- One large frypan plus lid
- One Dutch oven (which usually shares the frypan lid). Think this through. If you only use the electric frypan, you may not want to give space to this Dutch oven.
- One two-quart saucepan plus lid
- One one-and-one-half-quart saucepan plus lid
- One one-quart saucepan plus lid
- One electric griddle plus cord
- One electric frypan plus lid and cord
- One Crock Pot plus lid

If you're a quantity cooker, you may need an eight- to ten-quart kettle.

Ideally, pots should be stored with their lids on, but this is impractical for most kitchens. Next best is nesting them together and storing them beside the nested lids. If this won't work for you either, explore your cooking center space for a better way. Hanging as much as possible on inside cupboard walls and doors buys a lot of shelf space. Don't overlook the possibility of using screw-hooks to hang items from the undersides of interior shelves. However you deal with it, just remember to group like items together and keep only the basic cooking-related things in your cooking center.

For TRUE meals-in-minutes, keep your freezer stocked with "gravels." Home management expert Gloria Johnson suggests buying ground beef in large quantities for an extra savings. Then, after holding out what you need for meatloaf, meatballs, and patties, fry the remainder up, drain off the fat, and spread thin layers of the cooked and crumbled meat onto cookie sheets. Place these pans in the freezer to flash freeze the contents, then remove and put the frozen "gravel" into plastic freezer bags. This works well for sausage, too. Also buy cheese in bulk, grate, and freeze in freezer bags. Using this system, you always have the basic ingredients ready for a fast batch of anything that calls for cooked, ground beef . . . in minutes!

Seasonal cooking utensils like the turkey roaster, barbecue utensils, and canning equipment and supplies will be stored someplace else, away from prime kitchen space, probably in your designated storage area (see Chapter 15). Here's a tip regarding canning supplies: After a canning jar is emptied and washed, put a new lid on, upside down, plus the screw band, then store. This system keeps you one year ahead on all lids, and saves time and effort when you're canning because there's no need to hunt for and match lids to jars. It will also save you space—the new lids are stored on the jar, so there is no need to sacrifice space for lid storage. You will need a spot in your kitchen for a supply of canning lids (stored in a small box or drawstring bag)—preferably in a cleanup center drawer or under the sink. Be sure to number-code any boxes containing your seasonal kitchen storage things.

BAKING CENTER

This center involves an upper and lower cupboard; the countertop is used only as a work surface, not a resting place for canisters and the like. If you don't have upper or lower cupboard space for a baking center, you improvise. One woman we knew lived in a tiny mobile home that was painfully low on kitchen space. She had only four small upper cupboards, four small shallow drawers, and the space under her sink. (She was lucky enough to have a drawer in her stove, though.) So rather than devote the stove drawer to pots and pans, we put all the mixing bowls and all the bakeware there. This drawer approximated a lower cupboard and was close to her upper baking cupboard. Her pots, pans, and lids could be hung, so she hung them from floor to ceiling on the inside walls of a tiny broom closet that was next to her stove and close to the upper cooking cupboard.

Ideally, the baking center is located between the stove and sink. If you have a galley or corridor kitchen (that is, two banks of cupboards and appliances with a walkway between them), then locate the baking center next to the sink and directly opposite the stove. The other kitchen arrangements—L-shaped, U-shaped, and along one wall—also adapt to the baking center idea. (See illustrations and Kitchen Centers chart on the next six pages.)

The upper cupboard inventory of the baking center would include:

- All sweeteners (brown, powdered, and white sugar; corn syrup; honey; molasses; and so on)
- Shortening
- Vegetable oil (in small bottle)
- Flour
- Cornmeal

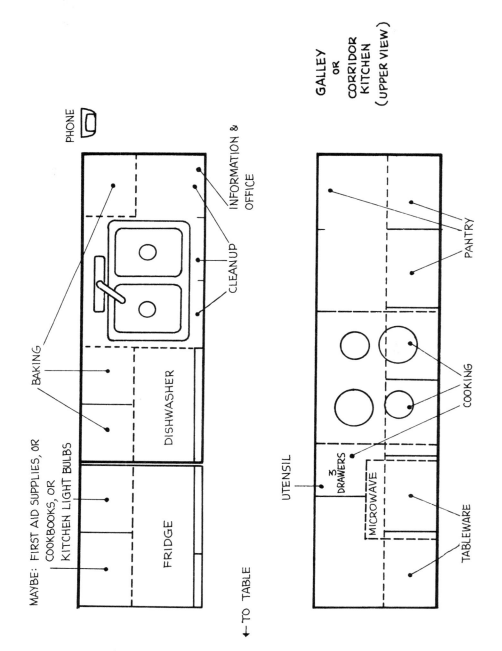

PHONE

INFORMATION &
OFFICE

CLEAN UP

BAKING

DISHWASHER

MAYBE: FIRST AID SUPPLIES, OR
COOKBOOKS, OR
KITCHEN LIGHT BULBS

FRIDGE

← TO TABLE

GALLEY
OR
CORRIDOR
KITCHEN
(UPPER VIEW)

PANTRY

COOKING

UTENSIL

3 DRAWERS

MICROWAVE

TABLEWARE

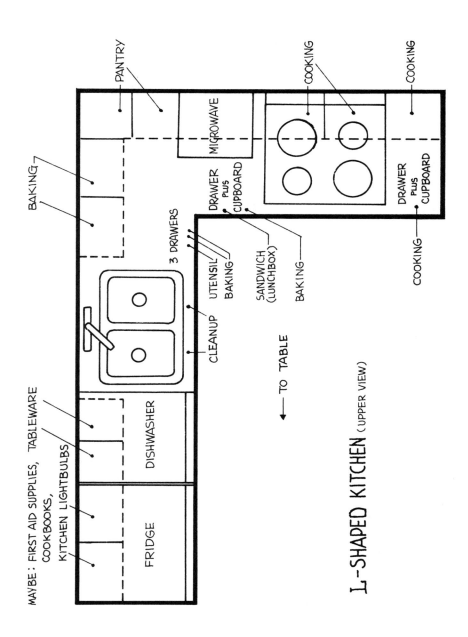

MAYBE: FIRST AID SUPPLIES, TABLEWARE
COOKBOOKS,
KITCHEN LIGHTBULBS

FRIDGE

DISHWASHER

CLEANUP

3 DRAWERS

← TO TABLE

PANTRY

MICROWAVE

DRAWER PLUS CUPBOARD

UTENSIL BAKING

SANDWICH (LUNCHBOX)

BAKING

COOKING

COOKING

DRAWER PLUS CUPBOARD

COOKING

BAKING

L-SHAPED KITCHEN (UPPER VIEW)

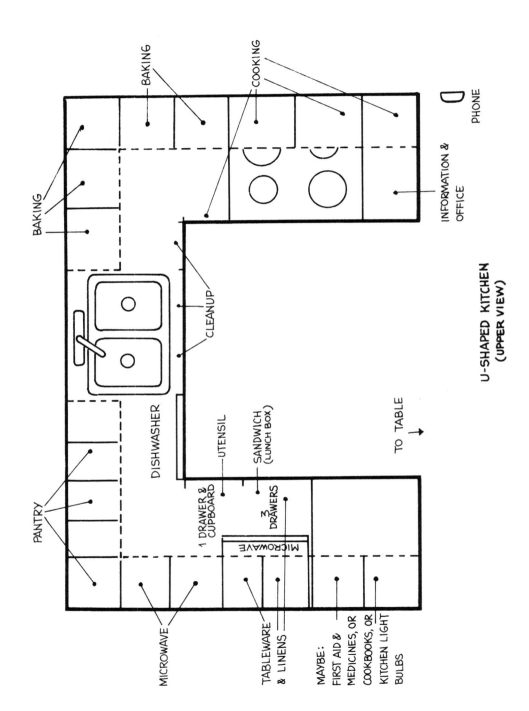

BAKING

BAKING

BAKING

COOKING

PHONE

INFORMATION &
OFFICE

CLEANUP

DISHWASHER

UTENSIL

SANDWICH
(LUNCH BOX)

PANTRY

1 DRAWER &
CUPBOARD

3
DRAWERS

TO TABLE

MICROWAVE

MICROWAVE

TABLEWARE
& LINENS

MAYBE:
FIRST AID &
MEDICINES, OR
COOKBOOKS, OR
KITCHEN LIGHT
BULBS

U-SHAPED KITCHEN
(UPPER VIEW)

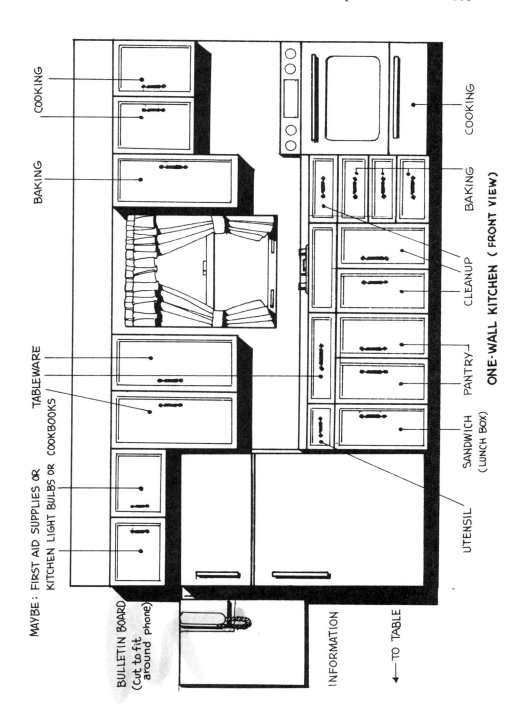

COOKING

COOKING

BAKING

BAKING

CLEANUP

TABLEWARE

PANTRY

MAYBE: FIRST AID SUPPLIES OR KITCHEN LIGHT BULBS OR COOKBOOKS

SANDWICH (LUNCH BOX)

UTENSIL

BULLETIN BOARD (Cut to fit around phone)

INFORMATION

← TO TABLE

ONE-WALL KITCHEN (FRONT VIEW)

KITCHEN CENTERS

CENTER:	Tableware	Cooking
Location:	In cupboard and drawer closest to table	In upper, lower cupboard and drawers next to stove
Basic Inventory:	dishes glassware serving bowls flatware table linens salt and pepper butter dish sugar bowl honey and jam pots syrup container trivets paper napkins paper plates and cups (seasonal) napkin rings	pastas cooking herbs salt and pepper cornstarch packaged mixes cooked cereals bouillon and hot-drink mixes garlic seasoned salt pot holders tongs wire whisk rubber spatula metal pancake turner wooden spoon large slotted spoon large spoon meat fork pots, pans plus lids Crock Pot griddle electric frypan parsley dried, chopped onions

CENTER:	Pantry	Microwave
Location:	Two shelves or separate pantry or closet at least near the kitchen	One or two shelves above, below, or near microwave
Basic: Inventory:	canned goods backup supplies (vegetable oil, salt box, and so on) dry cereals gelatins convenience mixes crackers	cooking and baking dishes (microwave-safe) thermometer carousel microwave cookbook recipes paper plates paper napkins

CENTER:	Office	
Location:	Shelf, drawer, or portable file box near table area; or built-in kitchen desk or other such designated room	
Basic Inventory:	pens and pencils address book stationery To Do file folder budget book small calendar	office supplies notebook paper stamps checkbook business-sized envelopes

CENTER:
Location:
	Baking
	Upper and lower cupboard including
	   counter between sink and stove
		Cleanup
		Sink and underneath cupboard,
		  plus one drawer to side of sink

Basic Inventory:	baking soda, baking powder all sweeteners shortening vegetable oil salt vanilla and other flavorings flour raisins, nuts, coconut oatmeal cocoa unsweetened chocolate baking chips spices toothpicks food colorings convenience mixes (cake, muffin, etc.) mixing bowls wooden spoon measuring spoons measuring cups one 4-cup measuring cup mixer and beaters rubber spatula pastry blender baking pans and sheets rolling pin and pastry cloth cooling racks cake-decorating equipment cookie cutters pastry brush	paper towels dish soap scouring pad plastic scouring pad dishwasher detergent dish drainer LinSol wood cleaner cleaning bucket cleaning cloths old toothbrush ammonia water in spray bottle oven cleaner 2- to 3-inch clean paintbrush 5 or 6 dishcloths 5 or 6 dish towels 4 or 5 hand towels 3 or 4 aprons new canning lids simple tool kit plunger (?) colander

CENTER:
Location:
	Sandwich
	Two shelves either above or below the
	  counter, or deep drawer(s)
		Information
		Drawer or shelf near phone, or the wall
		  surrounding the phone

Basic Inventory:	toaster bread goods peanut butter margarine lunch boxes plastic wraps other food wraps sandwich bags paper lunch sacks lunch box containers	phone book pen and pencil notepad *or* washable message board calendar tacks

- Baking soda
- Baking powder
- Salt (a container separate from those used for the tableware and cooking centers)
- Vanilla and other flavorings (in a container or on a turntable)
- Raisins
- Nuts (If space is limited, they also store well in the freezer.)
- Coconut
- Cocoa
- Oatmeal
- Baking chips
- Food colorings
- Spices (in a container such as a shoebox or plastic drawer organizer, or on a turntable)
- Toothpicks
- Mixes
- One four-cup liquid measuring container
- Mixing bowls (three graduated sizes, if there is room; otherwise, they will go in the bottom baking cupboard)

The upper cupboard inventory also includes a few utensils that can be hung on the door or inside wall, or from underneath a cupboard shelf from hooks:

- One wooden spoon
- One set measuring spoons
- One set measuring cups
- One rubber spatula
- Pastry blender
- Pastry brush
- Hand mixer plus cord (Examine any hand mixer and you'll find a built-in hole—it's made for hanging.)
- Beaters for hand mixer

The lower cupboard inventory should include:

- Baking pans and sheets
- Rolling pin and pastry cloth
- Cooling racks
- Large counter-type mixer plus attachments such as bread hook (Hang what you can, or store attachments in the large bowl that accompanies mixer.)
- Cake decorating equipment (in a container)
- Cookie cutters (in a container)

Note that we suggest using containers for several items. They encourage control. Shortening cans, old canisters, shoeboxes, baskets, and old lunch boxes are alternative suggestions to the usual store-bought type. Think "hang" and "containers" and buy yourself more space and control.

Speaking of baking: Save your six- and twelve-ounce frozen-juice cans. Fill them with a variety of cookie doughs, then cover the open tops with plastic wrap, secure with rubber bands, and freeze until baking time. When you're ready, let the mixture thaw a bit, then cut the bottom of the can off and use it to push dough up through the can for quick, even slicing.

CLEANUP CENTER

This area includes the sink, plus the cupboard directly underneath, and usually a drawer to one side of the sink. The sink needs no inventory: Remove everything from the top except for the two plugs. No more plastic scrubbers and scouring pads, no more gummy bars of soap, no more ratty dishrag, no more ceramic big-mouthed frog, and so on. These things go someplace else. This someplace else would probably be under the sink in a container (cleaning bucket or plastic dishtub, perhaps. Or the scrubber and dishrag could hang on the inside cupboard door or inside cupboard wall from small hooks or finishing nails. Any sink, porcelain or stainless steel, is easier to get clean and keep clean if it's clear—it looks nicer, too.

The purpose of the cleanup center is for more than washing dishes or storing household cleaners. It's also a place where fresh fruits and vegetables are handled, cooked pastas are rinsed and drained, canning jars are assembled for storage, and beverages are prepared. It's really a multipurpose center.

The underneath cupboard is a fun space to work with because you can really be clever here. With everything emptied out, this is the time to assess the space for usage potential. The typical sink cupboard is dark, damp, and loaded with too much stuff. Consider giving its walls and floor a coat of high-gloss, white enamel. This will brighten up the area and make cleaning easier. One of our clients went a step further and laid a cut-to-fit piece of Formica on the bottom of this cupboard.

Again, hang as much as possible on the inside of cupboard doors, on inside walls of cupboards, even from the underside of the countertop. A cleaning products shelf can be created from a board in the back of the cupboard.

Keep in mind that you probably don't need most of the cleaning products you currently stock. Take professional custodian Don Aslett's advice and buy four or five commercial plastic spray bottles; purchase your disinfectants and cleaners in concentrated gallons. (These can be found at any janitorial supply store.) Follow mixing directions given on container labels, and label each spray bottle. You'll get dollars' worth of cleaner for pennies an ounce, and the spray bottles will take up less space under your sink. Simply store the gallon jugs in your general storage area, described in Chapter 15. (For more nitty-gritty on cleaning, see the bathroom chapter.)

Streamlining your cleaning products collection will leave a lot of open space that will be put to better use. For example, sitting in a cleaning bucket under Alice's sink are a spray bottle of ammonia water, a commercial squeegee, an old toothbrush, a treated Maslin dustcloth (disposable, purchased at any janitorial supply house), a clean three-inch paintbrush, and five cleaning cloths. The ammonia water and squeegee are used for windows. The toothbrush cleans hard-to-get-at places like faucet crevices. The cleaning cloths, as opposed to tattered rags, are for the big, tough cleaning jobs like floor scrubbing. The paintbrush is great for dusting pleated lamp shades, mitered cupboard doors and picture frames, cupboard hardware, intricate woodwork, and so on. (For much more about cleaning, we refer you to several fine books listed under "Suggested Reading" at the end of this book.)

Basically, your under-sink inventory looks like this:

- Dish soap (Use a tiny squirt to wash your hands before handling food; this eliminates the need for gummy bar soap or a container of liquid soap—which is nothing more than expensive diluted dish detergent—on top of the sink.) If your sink is the community wash trough, consider rerouting others to the laundry or bathroom sinks for their grubby cleanup. Look at all areas of the kitchen in terms of food preparation and strict standards of sanitation. Keep the sink as clean and sanitary as possible.
- Dishwasher detergent
- Household cleaning products—the bare essentials. For safety reasons, you may want to put cleaners out of reach of little fingers, but if lack of space causes you to put them under the sink, childproof locks on the doors should keep this area secure.
- Good window squeegee
- Cleaning bucket, with aforementioned basic supplies tucked inside
- Dish drainer. Hang it on the inside wall or door, or stand it up along the side wall. If you've located your cleaners elsewhere, you might consider standing up flat items such as cookie and pizza pans, trays, and cutting

Under the sink is a good location for the Cleanup Center.

boards on their side next to the drainer, especially if you have no slotted tray cupboard; you can improvise a tray cupboard to fit the space under the sink.

- Colander(s), hung on the inside wall or door (Put a hole in the rim of the plastic type for hanging.)
- Plunger. You might want it under a bathroom sink if this cupboard must house the colander, flat baking pans, or trays. But whichever sink it sits under, it'll do so more easily if you shorten the handle.
- New canning lids in a small box or drawstring bag (which, of course, could be hung up)
- Simple tool kit (This could also sit in the cupboard over the refrigerator or in an empty drawer. Don't overlook the possibility of drawstring-bagging the contents.) The kit should include a screwdriver, a Phillips screwdriver, a pair of pliers, a small hammer, a small container of finishing nails, a picture-hanging kit or two, Super Glue, and wood glue.
- Shoeshine kit (This could also go in the utility or laundry area, depending on where shoes are shined; the bedroom, however, is not the greatest place for this dirty job.) Tuck some newspaper inside the container for use as a drop cloth.
- Paper towels could go on the inside of the door. A handier place may

be on the wall between the sink and microwave – one exception to the "nothing-on-the-work-area walls" doctrine.

- If there's no better out-of-the-way place for the garbage, then under the sink it goes, in a plastic container; a doorhung container is best, because it frees space on the cupboard floor.
- A nice dish cloth, dish towel, and hand towel hung on rods attached to the inside door (Another spot for these might be at the end of a bank of cupboards.)

The under-sink area is prone to overload, mostly because of cleaning products. So when you stock this area, work toward "efficient" rather than "full."

The drawer to the side of or near the sink holds:

- Six or seven dish cloths
- Six or seven dish towels
- A few decorative hand towels

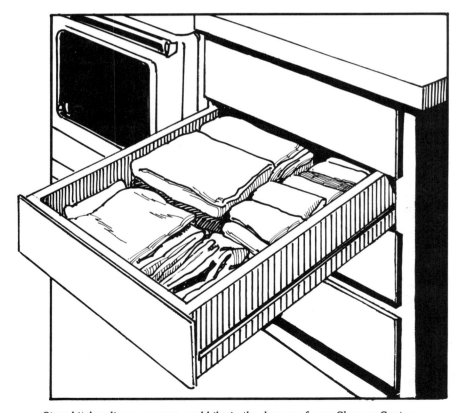

Store kitchen linens, aprons, and bibs in the drawer of your Cleanup Center.

- A couple of aprons
- Baby bibs, if this applies

If you lack drawer space, these items could rest neatly in a plastic dish tub under the sink.

PANTRY

This depends on available space and where you've housed your other centers; it's a minimal storage spot and not a work center, so the pantry area will use any leftover kitchen space, or it could even be in a closet close to the kitchen. (Streamlining makes such spaces available.) One phonebooth-sized kitchen we streamlined had no leftover space for the pantry, so the home manager installed shelves in the living room closet, immediately around the corner from the kitchen, and stocked it with backup supplies of staples.

This area is considered a minimal storage center because it usually is not big enough to hold bulk sizes or large quantities of things. It's the place for selected amounts of:

- Canned goods
- Dry cereals
- Crackers
- Convenience mixes
- Fruit-flavored gelatins
- A few backup supplies (salt box, large bottle of vegetable oil, five- to ten-pound sack of sugar, five- to ten-pound sack of flour, infrequently used herbs and spices, and so on)

Thinking of your pantry area as the place for your two- to three-week food supplies and the storage area as the place for longer-term food supplies will make it easier to position this center.

MORE FROM CENTRAL PLANNING

Your lifestyle determines the kinds of centers in your kitchen, so you'll pick and choose from this chapter. We have four more suggestions, though, that can add extra convenience and efficiency to any kitchen.

Microwave ovens have become standard equipment today—hence the need for a microwave center. Ideally, it should be located in a cupboard directly above or below your microwave if it's a countertop model. If you have a built-in wall microwave, the center would be in the closest adjacent cupboard. If your microwave is on a cart, put the center on the cart shelves directly underneath the appliance. This center houses:

- All microwave-style cooking and baking dishes
- Carousel
- Thermometer
- Paper plates and napkins
- Microwave cookbook and recipes

We once streamlined a kitchen that just didn't have an available cupboard to devote to microwave-only items. So we combined all the microwave dishes on a shelf in the tableware cupboard. (The home manager also uses these microwave dishes as her table serving dishes.)

A Sandwich or Brown-Bag Center needs a shelf or two, either above or below a counter, or a large deep drawer. It's handy if this center is located near the built-in cutting board, if you have one. This space must be large enough to accommodate:

- Toaster (Set it in a shoebox lid or some other improvised tray to catch crumbs. If a shoebox lid strikes you as tacky, you may want to find a metal tray of the same approximate size.)
- Bread goods
- Peanut butter (Note that the old-fashioned style can be stored up to a month without refrigeration if its storage area temperature is moderate.)
- Margarine
- Lunch box(es)
- Paper lunch sacks
- Food wraps and sandwich bags
- Lunch box containers (thermos, small serving cups with tight-fitting lids, and so on)
- Plastic flatware
- Paper napkins
- Small container of milk-money change and a pen or pencil for labeling the brown bags

Even if your lifestyle doesn't call for a sandwich or brown-bag center, you should keep the toaster off the counter. Putting it into a cupboard or deep drawer near the place you use it would be best. We've streamlined hundreds of kitchens, and in every instance, clients rated clear countertops as their favorite aspect of it all (an efficient baking center ranked second).

An Information Center is a requirement if your kitchen has a phone. Obviously, the center should be near the phone; it could be a drawer, shelf, or just

Use ingenuity to cope with lack of space when establishing your Information Center near the phone.

a cork bulletin board or washable message board. The items needed for this center are few. They include:

- Phone book
- Scheduling calendar
- Pencil
- Notepad for messages
- Tacks for posting messages

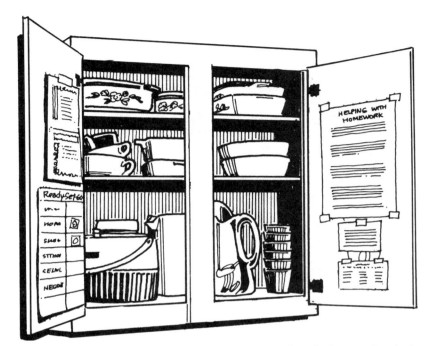

If space is scarce, extend your Information Center to cupboards that are close to the phone.

- Bulletin board *or* washable message board

Use your ingenuity here. If you have lots of drawer or shelf space, borrow some for this center. If there's no drawer or shelf, then the wall surrounding the phone is your answer (most kitchen phones are wall-mounted). One family surrounded their phone with sturdy corkboard out of which a phone-sized piece had been cut. This board was attached to the wall with a staple gun rather than glue, so it could be easily removed should the family change its mind about wanting a corkboard wall around their phone. If you use a corkboard as your message center, tack the notepad to the board; tape a string to a pencil and tack that and a calendar up also. If your phone book is small and it would be handier to hang it, then open it to the middle, lay a sturdy cord down the center of the back, shut the book, tie the two cord ends together, and you have looped your book for hanging.

If you just use a washable message board, the need for notepad and pencil is eliminated, but you'll still need a handy place for the calendar and phone book. Incidentally, don't slap a calendar, no matter how pretty the pictures, up on the wall as you would a framed picture. Calendars are service items and rarely do well as part of wall decor. Better to mount it inside a cupboard door, closet door, onto the bulletin board, or on the end of a bank of cupboards.

The Office Center is the last of our suggestions. This is a combination-location center: a trash can outside, a shelf or drawer near the table, or a portable file box and the kitchen table itself, unless you're one of the lucky ones with a built-in kitchen desk or separate office room. The outside trash can is where you deposit all junk mail before it enters the house, and your table or desk is where bill paying, checkbook balancing, menu planning, letter writing, and handling of *keeper* incoming mail take place. The shelf, drawer, or file box holds the necessary items for all this:

- Pen and pencil
- Address book
- Stationery
- Small calendar
- Notebook paper
- Checkbook (unless you keep it in your purse, in which case you'll retrieve it when doing your budgeting and book balancing)
- Office supplies
- To Do file folder
- Budget book

The To Do file folder is the place to put bills that need paying, letters that need answering, and the food ads from the current week's newspaper (unless you can deal with these immediately after the arrival of the newspaper). These grocery sale ads will help you compose your weekly menu. If chicken is on sale, for example, then chicken is a logical choice for an evening meal, the weekend barbecue, and perhaps for sandwiches for one day's lunches. If there's a good buy on bananas, then this is what you'll buy plenty of, rather than lots of apples, which could be considerably more expensive. From this weekly menu, you will write your grocery list. This is a slick system because you'll not only save money by avoiding impulse and desperation purchases, but you'll also save on in-store time — no more wandering and pondering what to fix for dinner tonight.

The papers brought in with your school-aged children don't go there, however. Deal with school papers as soon as they enter the house, or as soon as you enter the house. To avoid paper pile-up, don't fall into the trap of *habitually* saving children's school papers. If you'll notice, at report card and conference time the teacher usually sends home the best-of-the-best of the child's work that *she* has sorted out. (If she doesn't do this, ask her to.) Save these pieces along with the year's report cards (in the treasure box) and you have a good representation of your child's academic growth and development for that year. Meanwhile, display the current week's work on your laundry or sewing area wall. Of course, if something extra special does come home, such as the plaster-of-paris handprint, the hand-fashioned clay dinosaur, or other unusual art-work, you may want to find a permanent display spot for it. Alice displays a framed oil painting of a house-flowers-smiling-sun-happy-boy scene that her nineteen-year-old son Andrew painted when he was six. Alice's husband, Gordon, displays all the clay animals their children have made over the years on the credenza in his office. So the school days "treasures" do have a place in your life and home, but be highly selective and realistic.

Have children wash out and dry their lunchboxes while you're looking their things over. Then sign what needs signing, tuck it into the clean lunch box (or their backpack pocket) to be transported the next day, and forget about it. (This technique takes care of the "Hurry and sign my papers, the bus is coming!" scramble that so many mornings can witness.)

While we're not experts on papers and filing, we think this tip bears repeating: On the way into the house with the mail, stop off at the trash can to deposit all junk mail. This keeps the in-house paper piles much smaller. And here's one final idea for controlling junk mail blight: Consider having your name removed from ALL junk mailing lists by writing to:

Mail Preference Service
Direct Mail Marketing Association
6 E. Forty-third St.
New York, NY 10017

And SAVE A TREE!

LEFTOVERS THAT AREN'T OVERLOAD

There are five categories of kitchen items that still need some attention. First of all, your general utensils need a home all their own. (General utensils are anything you don't cook or bake with, such as the hand can opener, ice cream scoop, nutcracker, pie server, bottle opener, and so on.) If there's an empty drawer, then in they go, probably in a drawer organizer. If there isn't an empty drawer, group them into a container, and find a vacant spot in some already occupied drawer.

Some words on the electric can opener: If you love it and routinely use it, keep it—but keep it off the counter. You will find some drawer it can sit in or some shelf or cupboard it can sit on. Even if you use it fourteen times a day, we still say get it off the counter. Clear surfaces are worth any inconvenience created: They make for easy maintenance, allow your decorator touches to finally be noticed, make a room look cleaner and bigger, instill vigor, inspiration, and enthusiasm . . . . Need we go on? If you don't use it regularly and feel you could get along with the hand can opener, fine – discard the electric one. (As you can see, we don't advocate electric can openers . . . to us they are space wasters!)

Next, what about knives and other cutting tools, such as the cheese slicer or pizza wheel? Don't hang them on the wall or set them in a knife block on the counter. If they are keepers, put them in a drawer, *in containers,* perhaps in their own cardboard sleeves (for blade and sharpness preservation).

Third, what to do with all those plastic bowls and lids? First of all, sort through them and keep only four or five plus matching lids, in graduated sizes. All should be in tip-top shape. When these bowls are full of leftovers, then it's time to empty them out and serve what we call a "Good Luck with Our Potluck" dinner.

Rather than nest these bowls inside one another and plop the lids somewhere else, place a lid on each bowl and stack them, two bowls per stack, or whatever your cupboard space allows. They will sit neatly in a cupboard (the best place is near the cleanup center or refrigerator). Keep them separate from serving and mixing bowls.

What about cookbooks and recipes? After you've streamlined these, too, place the keepers in or near one of several places: the baking center, the cooking center, or the office center (if this center is in the kitchen).

Finally, what do you do with the broom, dustpan, and mop? Most people own this equipment, yet most homes have little or no space to accommodate them. The ideal would be a cleaning or janitorial closet just off the kitchen, large enough to house all your cleaning machines and supplies. But since this ideal is rarely realized, we have some alternative suggestions.

- If you have a door between the garage and the kitchen, hang them on the garage wall, just outside the door.
- If there's access to the wall behind the refrigerator, pull the refrigerator out three and a half to four inches and hang the items up behind the refrigerator. Use spring-type clamps for the broom and mop; hang the wisk broom and dustpan from hooks inserted into the underside of the cupboard above the refrigerator, if there is one. The same principle applies if there's access to a side wall beside the refrigerator.
- If there is a hall closet off the kitchen (maybe the guest coat closet), designate one end wall as the broom and mop center and hang these things there.
- If there's a stairway off the kitchen leading down to the basement or cellar, hang the broom, mop, dustpan, and so forth on one stairway wall. The exception to this idea, however, is if this stairway is a main traffic artery

leading to a live-in basement, such as one with a family room and/or bedrooms. In this case, due to the aesthetics and visual clutter concept, you'd find another place for your floor cleaning gear.

- Wherever you put them, be sure to hang them up. This is cleaner, more convenient, and it preserves broom bristles.

TAKE NOTE

It's helpful to understand, as you're assigning things to each center, that there are four categories of utensils in a kitchen: cooking (such as the meat fork and large slotted spoon), baking (such as measuring cups and pastry blender), cutting (such as the electric knife, cheese slicer, paring knives, and kitchen shears), and general (such as the hand can opener, ice cream scoop, and bottle opener).

There are four categories of bowls in a kitchen: serving (which are usually glass or ceramic), mixing (which are usually plastic, glass, or metal), microwave-safe (which are usually glass and ceramic), and refrigerator storage (which are also glass, plastic, or metal and have matching lids). As you can see, the utensil or bowl type will dictate where each should be stored.

While filling trash and charity bags, consider putting quality duplicates and extra items into an "apartment box" if you have someone in the family who will eventually strike out on his or her own. This box would be labeled and placed in storage until needed.

LAST BUT NOT LEAST

With everything streamlined, centers pinpointed and stocked, and leftovers taken care of, it's time to deal with walls. As we stated earlier, the kitchen is the place to keep things extra simple. Put nothing on work area walls. Hang nothing along your soffits. This means less to clean, less time needed for maintenance, less clutter, less visual confusion.

If you enjoy decorator touches such as baskets, plants, pottery, brass or copper, and so on, here and there in your kitchen, remember what we said in the living room chapter: Decorative accents get buried in clutter. Keep the kitchen streamlined, and your decorating will be easily noticed and will really enhance the room.

As for the rest of the kitchen walls, use the basic principles of design. You and your family spend lots of time in the kitchen, so take this opportunity to create a visually inspiring and work-conducive kitchen — one that really "measures up."

ELEVEN

CABINETS, CLOSETS, AND CUPBOARDS

Streamlining
these crucial storage areas

C abinets, closets, and cupboards are almost interchangeable in function, and they're very close by definition, too. According to *Webster's* dictionary, a cabinet is a case or cupboard, usually with doors and shelves. A cupboard is a closet with shelves, usually where dishes, utensils, appliances, or food is kept. And a closet is a cabinet or recess for china, household utensils, or clothes. We would add that cabinets, closets, and cupboards are the skeleton of the home – the framework upon which the surface appearance of room interiors depends.

Whatever you call these indispensable storage zones – and that varies by region and family – they're probably very full of all the things mentioned in those definitions, and more. Before we streamlined our homes, we were constantly struggling for control of our storage areas. We found, however, that it wasn't enough just to organize their contents; we had done that repeatedly and realized that this temporary type of organization wasn't the answer. We were doing the household shuffle, when all along we should have been using the household shovel. A poem from the pen of one of our seminar attendees, Fran Spooner, describes the situation well:

Trying to find
Boggles my mind.
I know it's in there . . .
But where!?
Pawing through
The closet that grew . . .
Makes me think it needs roto-rootering,
Or better yet, how about neutering?

We needed a system that would give us control of our closets and all other spaces in our homes once and for all. Here, as elsewhere in the house, streamlining *then* organizing is the answer. And because you're dealing with relatively small spaces, streamlining is all the more vital.

You will find that the cabinets, closets, and cupboards you use the most will need frequent streamlining. Other, less frequently used spaces will stay streamlined for six months or more. Also, cabinets, closets, and cupboards that are loaded with too much—even with too many keepers—still prove overwhelming to children. Thus these areas must be streamlined to the bare bones and set up with the most child-oriented efficiency possible. (Labeling specific areas may be helpful here.)

HALL CLOSETS

Treat hall or hall-type closets just as you would the master bedroom or other bedroom closets. It doesn't matter whether the items in it are coats, china, games, or cleaning supplies. Here are some general pointers.

Where is it and what is it for? Note the closet's location and determine its purpose. Evaluate it with convenience and availability in mind. A closet near the front door is probably not the best place for your twice-a-year camping equipment, if that's the only entrance-level closet you have. The space is needed more for coats. If you have a back-door or basement closet, that's a better place for the camping goods; if you don't, consider the garage (and see Chapter 15 for more about that).

Do you like, use, need, want, or have room for it? Touch every item in the closet and apply these key questions. Why give prime space—or any space—to things we don't like, don't use, don't need, don't want, and really don't have room for? Don't be tempted to keep inferior items. Limited space should be used for only high quality things. By weeding out nonessentials, you'll find far less to organize. Quality over quantity is always the motto.

Gamesmanship. Some prefer to keep all the games in a central location. If this is where you've decided to put boardgames and puzzles, rather than in the children's rooms, then deal with them just as discussed in Chapter 7. Assess their condition and determine if they are worth keeping. Check for broken or missing pieces, which will never return; decide too, whether the games are still of interest to anyone. This type of assessment could whittle down your game and puzzle collection by half.

Group and store like items together. For instance, gather up all costumes or children's play dress-up items and store them in one box; collect all your arts, crafts, and needlework projects and put them into one container. Here's a time- and money-saving tip: Keep a box for "gifts"; fill it with all-age, all-occasion prewrapped gifts (each one discreetly labeled with a tie-on tag so you won't forget what it is). These gifts will most likely be quality, after-season sale items. This system ends that last-minute gift hunt we all know and dread.

Must return. This may be a handy location for a Must Return basket or box.

Food and home-management storage from freed space.

By removing some shelves you create an automatic sports center.

"Must return" things are all the items you've borrowed or that were inadvertently left behind by visitors, such as overdue library books, the bag of powdered sugar you owe the next-door neighbor, the pattern for Aunt Lily's afghan, your pastor's umbrella, and so on. Grouping and storing all "must return" items together increases the likelihood of their being returned and protects them from being damaged or lost until they are.

Pack it up. Store seasonal things out of the way. This frees space for things of the current season. We once streamlined a closet that was hiding garden seeds, ski boots, hiking backpacks, and a steam canner. We grouped these things with other related items and packed them away, waiting for the correct season to call them forth.

Put it where you use it. Store frequently used items in handy places – at their point of use whenever possible. For example, we use our mixer/dough-hook/blender appliance three or four times a day, so we need it in a convenient cupboard, out front for quick removal. We use our curling irons and blow dry-ers at least once every day, so we have them hanging on the inside of the bath-room cabinet door for easy access. We use our typewriters every day, but we use our slide projector only three or four times a month in seminars. So you can see which items belong in prime, convenient spaces.

It's not always possible to have everything at your fingertips, of course. A little inconvenience may be necessary – but at least store the item as near as possible to its logical place-of-use spot.

Put it back where you found it! Be fanatical with everyone about putting things back in their assigned spots. Neglect of this can undo any organizational system. This is a realistic expectation once there are plenty of empty spaces and logical assignments for all keepers. Once, it might not have been fair to expect your five-year-old to put the Candyland game away; even you probably couldn't squeeze another game box onto the game shelf without it falling on your head. Fear of toppling shelves and exploding drawers prevented everyone but the most fearless from attempting to put things back where they were pulled from. But this isn't the case anymore.

However, when a case of the "lazies" hits and folks just can't seem to muster the strength to put things back where they found them, we discipline by remov-ing the privilege of using said item(s) for a while. ("A while" depends on how chronic this problem is.) You might also consider "black bagging" everything you have to pick up; all owners must pay a fixed amount to get their things back (this should include adults, too). Whatever enforcement measures you choose, you can see that consistency is the key here.

Hang in there! Be sure to hang as much as possible. Look at the space within the closet – along the back wall, closet ceiling, and other inside walls. These may be feasible areas to hang related items that aren't frequently used but do belong in the closet. For instance, Alice grouped poster paints into a drawstring bag and hung them from the closet ceiling, above the oil-paints box and glue gun kit that sit on the upper shelf.

MORE NO-LINEN-CLOSETOLOGY

Here's a revolutionary thought: You may not really *need* a linen closet for extra bed linens. Storing them in a linen closet is an extravagant waste of space. In the interest of better space management, get rid of the extra bed linens.

We can't think of a single home we've ever been in that didn't have a linen closet or cupboard, so we conclude that linen closets are an integral ingredient

in the American housing concept. This probably explains why we run into opposition when we introduce this different approach to linen storage. It sounds
radical at first, but it frees needed space.

Here's what you do. After assessing the condition of all bed linens and discarding any that are worn or faded (perhaps saving a few in the garage rag bag),
pack the rest into a box and store it. Keep only what is currently on the beds,
plus an extra set laid flat between box spring and mattress. (If you have a waterbed, store the extra set on the closet shelf or in a drawer.) You may decide to
assign a certain color of sheets to each bedroom. If you have small children or
a bed-wetter, store a couple sets of sheets laid flat between the mattresses. Even
an extra blanket will store well between the mattresses if you lay it flat. When
it's time to launder, take the bed linens off, wash and dry them, then return
them to their appropriate places. This extra set between the box spring and
mattress is basically for emergencies or to be put on the mattress if you can't
get the dirty set laundered and put back on in the same day. For a Hide-A-Bed,
use the same approach: Store a set of sheets and a blanket flat between the
folded-up mattress sections, or place the clean bedding directly on the mattress, and store it in the folded-up Hide-A-Bed. If you have extra pillows, box
them up and store them away.

There are many uses for extra sheets besides the garage rag bag. (Although
we don't recommend using rags for house cleaning, they're great for other
messy projects such as painting, changing the oil in the car, and refinishing
furniture.) Old sheets make great costumes, first-aid kit bandages (when ripped
into strips and sterilized), drop cloths, and drawstring bags.

Somewhere in the middle of our No-Linen-Closetology speech we are often
interrupted with one or both of these comments: "But if the linens aren't rotated, they'll wear out quicker," and "But that's boring. I like a variety of sheets."
In reply to the first objection, we do not have any specific information to refute
it. In fact, it's probably true. But we reason that having the extra, streamlined
closet space is well worth having the sheets wear out a little sooner. We're convinced this "necessary" linen closet could be put to better use. To the second
comment we just can't relate. We'd rather have clear, uncluttered space than a
variety of sheets. The choice is yours.

Here are some suggestions for space that used to be a linen closet. We recognize that not everyone has a main floor linen closet; because closet locations
are so variable, the usefulness of these ideas will depend on the floor plan of
your home.

Give your arts and crafts a home. Turn it into an arts-and-crafts center, or
keep your sewing machine, serger, supplies, and notions there.

Corral your hobbies. Establish a hobby center. One of our clients, an avid
wood-carver, keeps her scores of knives, chisels, gouges, and clamps on one

Sewing closet.   *Canning and canned goods closet.*

shelf, and her vast assortment of wood blocks on another shelf. The remaining shelves hold her patterns, instruction and idea books, sandpapers, projects-in-progress, and so on.

Create career-centered storage. It can serve as an extension of your job. One grade school teacher we know turned her linen closet into an alternate storage area for her classroom. Here she keeps labeled boxes of bulletin board materials, arts and crafts supplies, a case of finger paint powders, classroom holiday decorations, party favors and paper goods, stacks of idea files, and so on. Having a storage area away from her classroom allows her to visually and physically free up some classroom space in what was previously a crowded and overloaded room.

We also know a piano teacher who has no space for a freestanding file cabinet, so she uses her linen closet as a master file cabinet for her massive collection of sheet music, lesson books, composition and theory papers, and related items.

Give order to books. Turn it into a minilibrary. If you have no shelves, or no space for shelves in any of your other rooms, yet you have a large assortment of books that you would like to use and display, this may be the place to do it. By removing the door or doors to this closet, you now have a convenient, efficient, yet out-of-the-way center for books.

Create a minioffice. Alice, for example, does all her writing at the kitchen table, but stores her files, reference books, copies of *Writer's Digest* magazine, paper, pencils, and so on in the former linen closet.

Establish a children's library/school-book center. One mother, whose children share tiny bedrooms, needed an orderly spot for each child's collection of library books and school books. We emptied the linen closet and assigned one shelf to each child.

Create a home interiors center. We've seen a number of home managers who enjoy decorating their homes throughout the entire year (not just for Christmas or Hanukkah) use this area as their holiday/seasonal decor center. Here is where they conveniently house their table centerpieces, seasonal door and hearth wreaths, novelty candles, and so forth.

Make a gift center. This would be the place to keep the box of prepurchased, prewrapped, prelabeled gifts mentioned earlier. This would also be the spot for your collection of all-occasion gift wraps and ribbons, gift cards, an assortment of bubble-lined mailers, gift boxes, lining tissues, brightly colored gift bags, cellophane tape, scissors, string, and a booklet on creative gift wrapping.

Establish a china and crystal center. If you lack dining room storage space, you might find that a china and crystal center would work well here.

Make a beverage/entertainment center. One of our clients converted his linen closet to a wine/liquor/entertainment center, which freed up a tremendous amount of space in his kitchen.

Create a food center. If you're tight on food storage space, keeping food here may be the answer, either for long-term storage or as an off-kitchen pantry.

Establish an upstairs, off-the-bedrooms study or craft area. An upstairs linen closet can be converted to an arts and crafts center, a library-study center (by installing a table-height shelf, an electrical outlet for a lighting fixture, and a small stool).

Make an upstairs, off-the-bedrooms toy center. Often children's bedrooms are too small to efficiently house toys. By removing them from the room, you free up space for essentials such as a bed, dresser, desk, or hobby table.

CHINA CABINETS OR DINING ROOM BUILT-INS

This spot can be one of the loveliest in the home if it isn't overloaded or used as a drop-off station. Unfortunately, it is here that we've found piles of ratty tablecloths and placements, wrinkled gift-wrapping paper, melted-beyond-use candles, and drawers full of papers needing filing. Completely unload it and assess every item, firmly using the key questions.

So that this area can be an efficient amenity rather than a complete detraction, give each cabinet section a specific assignment and then reload it accordingly. Depending on its location, it might serve as your tableware center, thus freeing up needed kitchen cupboard and drawer space.

You may find that once you have your china or dining cupboard streamlined, you'll be inclined to use your pretty things on a regular basis, rather than waiting for those few special occasions. Not only is this a fun family treat (breakfast juice in goblets, ketchup in the crystal jam dish, and so on), but it encourages better table manners and affords you the opportunity to experience daily routines with a flourish.

Thanks to the Clutter Therapy of streamlining, a once-sick skeleton can now stand up to the surface neatness "acid test" of guests opening the wrong door or cupboard. And what's even more exciting, the framework of your home, the cabinets, closets, and cupboards, can now become assets rather than liabilities—oh, to think of the world of improvements your home can embody just by having a healthy skeleton!

TWELVE

MY SOAP OPERA

Eliminate the drama, the tears, the tragedy
of your wash-day routine
by streamlining your laundry area

Washing machines don't really eat socks. And dirty socks don't really get up and walk away. But when desperate searches throughout the house turn up nothing, you do begin to wonder. Creating a more efficient (and naturally more pleasant) laundry area will do a lot to solve that recurring mystery.

A laundry area can fulfill many functions, but the foremost is to wash and dry laundry. Because laundry is a never-ending, cyclic chore, it's crucial that the place in which you spend so much time be a cheerful and efficient work center, and not a demoralizing, unproductive torture chamber.

After careful study of many laundry centers, we've come up with this composite sketch of a typically overloaded, inefficient wash-dry spot (see if you relate to any of this):

- Broken, dilapidated laundry baskets, or NO laundry baskets
- Dirty laundry piled all over the floor
- Poor lighting
- Crowded, cluttered dryer top
- Cluttered windowsill
- Dirty window
- Bedraggled window curtain or covering, or no curtain or covering
- Laundry supplies crammed here and there
- Collections of assorted "empties" around
- Overflowing trash container or no trash container
- Inadequate or nonexistent shelving
- Illogically stocked, overloaded shelves
- Very dusty, dirty machines
- Dirty and dusty floors and windowsill
- Dirty and dusty hot water tank and furnace
- Bare walls except for fuse box and spider webs

- ✔ Dirty laundry sink with an assortment of laundry additive containers sitting in and/or on it
- ✔ A collection of orphaned screws, bolts, nails, pennies, rocks, marbles, crayons, school assignment sheets folded into tiny squares to fit in back pockets . . .
- ✔ Non-laundry-related clutter, such as a case of tuna, three bottles of anti-freeze, the dog leash, a soccer ball, the cat litter box, the box of Christmas lights . . .

Even the most expensive home is likely to have a laundry center that suffers from inefficient organization and a lifeless appearance. And that contributes to discouragement and irritation over a job that's never done and a place that's unpleasant to be in. Well, laundry will always be with us, so we need to make the best of it. Accepting drab, dirty, inefficient working conditions is unprofessional and sad. Here's our message of home managing hope: Something *can* be done about it—there's no need to live with a substandard laundry system. A thorough streamlining and cleaning of your laundry area will not only save you time and professionalize your wash-day routine, but also lift your spirits.

What condition is your laundry facility in, and how close to (or far from) the ideal is it? And what is the ideal, anyway? Well, the ideal is a clean, streamlined, bright, functional area with caught-up laundry. Even if your laundry setup suffers from a poor location (such as in the garage) and does double duty, sharing space with sink and toilet, miscellaneous storage, or a sewing machine, for example, it is possible to achieve this ideal. Try these ideas:

- Make sure the area is well lighted.
- Keep the windowsill clear for easy cleaning.
- Check the window covering: If it isn't attractive and serviceable, then change it.
- Don't use the dryer as a catchall. Keeping it clear and sparkling works magic on the area's overall appearance.
- Create a central laundry supply area, by installing shelving or cupboards. Having supplies grouped together in one spot will save time by streamlining your routine.
- If there is no shelf available in your laundry area, use hanging wire baskets to hold laundry supplies above the washer. Or add a shelf or cupboard if there is space available for one.
- Create a permanent spot for a continuously filling charity bag. Clothes are a transient affair—always in the process of wearing out, going out of style, or being outgrown. The laundry area is a logical place to do regular clothes assessment. Don't wait until closets and dressers are bulging with

A laundry area doesn't have to be big or custom built to be efficient. Rather, it simply needs shelves for supplies, a clear dryer top, and sparkling-clean surfaces.

obvious candidates for the charity bag—take care of them as they pass through the laundry.

- Use laundry baskets (in good condition) for sorting laundry rather than piling it on the floor. Or try using tall plastic kitchen trash containers for sorting soiled clothing—they don't take up as much floor space.
- Have a small basket handy to catch all the pocket paraphernalia that passes through the wash undetected—things like loose change, nails, crayons, folded school papers, and so on.
- Accommodate the miscellaneous laundry activities that are a regular feature of family life. For instance, set up a specific spot for deodorizing your teenager's stinky hightops. Create a place to hang the damp, just-out-of-the-washer 100 percent cottons, rather than tossing them into the dryer. (The dryer sets wrinkles, making ironing twice as time consuming.) As we hang, we hand press, removing as many of the wrinkles as possible while the garment is damp.
- Keep a spray bottle of highly diluted ammonia water solution and a cleaning cloth with your laundry supplies. This is good for wiping and shining the machines, hot water tank, and furnace. Keep a bottle of clear vinegar with laundry supplies. Add one half cup to one whole cup to the final rinse of the wash load once in a while; it cuts soap buildup.
- Linsol and Murphey's Oil Soap are terrific de-spotters and degreasers. Dilute them into a spray bottle of water (about two tablespoons into a twenty-two-ounce bottle) and use on all permanent press, 100 percent cottons, and denims.
- Keep a small mending kit near the machines for quick fix-ups, such as tacking a loose hem or restoring that missing collar button. This could be hung in a drawstring bag.

- Regularly dust and shine all surfaces in the area, including the hot water tank and furnace. This is especially important if the wash is done in the garage—you need as much sparkle in there as you can get.
- Periodically move machines for a thorough floor vacuuming and scrubbing. Go after those elusive dust bunnies.
- If yours is a sock-eating machine, try two things: Load the socks first, and/or have everyone put dirty socks in their own net bag (either purchased or home sewn). Then just toss socks, bag and all into the machine; they'll come clean without losing mates. Alice made her net bags about the size of a pillow case since most of her children wear the large, heavy-duty tube and athletic socks. Each person is then responsible for pairing up his or her own socks. (Keep the empty sock bags hanging on a hook inside each bedroom closet, or on a hanger next to the hanging laundry bag, to await more dirty socks.)
- Once your home is streamlined, allow mateless socks to linger only a few weeks. If mates don't show up after about a month, junk them and start

Make your own cover from an old sheet or other large piece of fabric. The pattern is the shape of your board, plus 8 inches all around to accommodate the cover wrapping across the top and under the top, plus a 2-inch casing for the elastic. The length of elastic inserted into the 2-inch casing should be about three fourths the entire circumference of the board shape. Example: If it is 65 inches around the outside of the board, the elastic length would be 41¼ inches. Thread the elastic through the casing, stitch ends, and slip the casing over the old cover and pad.

over with new pairs of socks. (This mismatch business is why we always buy the same size and color socks for every child in our families. Matching socks is an insane time-waster!)

- If there are lots of beds in your house, assign one day of the week to laundering the bedding of one or two at a time. This way you avoid that grueling chore of washing a mountain of bedding.
- Hang the ironing board up.
- If you buy your detergent in bulk, keep a smaller container of it in the laundry area and house bulk boxes in your storage area, unless there's ample, efficient space for backup laundry supplies in your laundry area.
- Here's a clean laundry idea that we admit isn't original (we first heard it from home management specialist Daryl Hoole). Have a labeled laundry tub (which can be a square plastic dish tub or a plastic kitty litter box) for each person in the family. This is where all clean, folded laundry goes. Assign to each individual the responsibility of putting his or her own folded clothes away and returning the empty tubs to the laundry area.
- Speaking of folding laundry, if at all possible, fold all laundry in the laundry area—not on the bed, or the living room or family room couch. Somehow it never gets put away fast enough to beat the unexpected drop-in visitors.
- Make a place for hair-cutting implements, including a dust pan and small shop broom for the after-cut cleanup.
- Hang a bulletin board nearby so you can post a stain removal chart, fabric care labels, and so on.
- Consider hanging the children's Mother's Day and Christmas cards and gifts on a laundry area wall. This brightens things up, and children enjoy seeing their work displayed.
- Baby toys, Fisher Price Little People, and other small washable toys can be sanitized in the washing machine. Set the machine on the gentle cycle, use hot water and bleach with the detergent. Add two or three bath towels to cushion the ride.
- In conclusion, one last laundry tip: Keep a sense of humor, especially if there are kids in the house. And if laundry ever gets the best of you, look at it this way: The beauty of living out of the dryer is that it saves space (you don't need dressers) and money (you don't need to buy laundry tubs!).

THIRTEEN

NO MORE SO-SO SEWING AREA

Creating a sewing haven

Aseparate room for sewing is every sewer's dream, but it's not always a possibility. Some have only part of a room; others have only a closet for storing the machines, notions, and fabric, and a kitchen table to sew on. Wherever *you* sew, this chapter is for you.

We love to sew and quilt, have done it for years, and know what it's like to work in an overloaded sewing area. We also know that overload and the resulting clutter and confusion can cure you of a love of sewing and quilting.

If you're in danger of that kind of cure—if yours is only a so-so sewing area (or not even that)—here are some ways you can streamline and improve it.

STREAMLINE YOUR PATTERNS

Start with your patterns. Watch these, because they pile up fast and go out of style faster. Only keep patterns that have all the pieces, that you *like*, and that are classic styles. A classic style is one that routinely reappears on the fashion scene, such as the dirndl skirt, the straight skirt, the wraparound skirt, and the pleated skirt. With an up-to-date fabric choice and a current hem length, these patterns can be used and reused for years. The shirtwaist dress, tuxedo blouse, pajamas, nightgown and robe, are other examples of timeless patterns. You'll notice infants' and children's patterns are all pretty basic, with only the fabric choice and decorative touches establishing a "new" seasonal look. Once you've determined your keepers, file them in a drawer or cardboard box. Use divider tabs labeled according to your particular sewing habits. For example:

Children's sizes	0-6
Children's	6-10
Girls' (or boys')	10-14
Girls' (or boys')	14-18
Men's	all sizes
Women's	all sizes

(Dresses, Sportswear, Maternity, Blouses and Tops)
Quilting
Miscellaneous

Under "Miscellaneous," file patterns for aprons, hats, costumes, doll clothes, home interior accessories, crafts, and needlework.

STREAMLINE AND FOLD YOUR FABRIC

Carefully evaluate your fabric supply. Keep only fabric that will look good after it's sewn. If it has permanent creases, faded or unfashionable colors, out-of-style fabric content, or is otherwise objectionable or flawed, get rid of it. For example, Alice once bought a pretty piece of single-knit fabric at a terrific price, brought it home, and discovered a large hole and run in the center of the piece. There was not enough fabric surrounding the hole and run to be useful, unless she was making knit potholders, which she wasn't. Of course, she kept this piece around for years; after all, she paid good money for it.

Some fabrics rot if kept too long, so watch for this also. When you are deciding what materials to store, remember that cotton blends (especially floral calico, gingham check, stripes, pin-dots, and plaid prints), denims, corduroy, flannel, muslin, and nylon tricot are classic fabrics. They are worth saving and storing. Other fabrics, such as knits and 100 percent polyesters, don't share this longevity, so don't give them long-term space. Whether you store your fabric in a drawer, on a shelf, or in a cardboard box, wash it first (to eliminate future shrinking problems), then indicate the yardage on each piece, so you can tell at a glance how much you have.

If you're a true-blue quilter, you will want any fabric destined for quilts labeled as such. Small swatches being saved for pieced and appliqué work should be sorted according to color families and placed in labeled manila envelopes, shoeboxes, or plastic Zip-loc bags.

Finally, if you're an avid seamstress, keep a small swatch booklet of your sewn fabric in your purse. For example, you could string these tiny pieces onto a large safety pin. You may even want to include little snips from the seams of your store-bought, ready-to-wear purchases. Then, when you are shopping (whether for additional fabric, additional ready-to-wear, shoes, or accessories), you can accurately match and coordinate all items in your wardrobe.

STREAMLINE AND NEATEN YOUR NOTIONS

Organize thread according to colors; do the same with bobbins. Storing thread and bobbins together rather than tossing bobbins in with machine attachments is a long-range time-saver. Grouping thread according to purpose is also helpful. (For instance, we have hand-quilting thread, machine embroidery thread, buttonhole twist, and invisible hemming thread. All this was hard to keep track of when mixed in with general purpose thread. Grouping threads was a big help.)

After evaluating your sewing notions, group the keepers together according to kind and store each group in its own container. Baby food jars, bouillon cube containers, even plastic sandwich bags make good containers for grouped sewing notions.

Streamline your zipper collection, too, and put what's left in labeled plastic Zip-loc bags, labeled shoeboxes, or manila envelopes; sort zippers according to length and kind, rather than color. The entire assortment could then be stored in another larger, labeled container. Be practical with zippers. We used to buy our notions in bulk at a fabric outlet, where zippers were so many cents a pound. Because they were such a fantastic buy, we'd buy anything and everything. So we ended up with placket zippers when what we needed were dress and skirt zippers, heavy-duty metal-toothed zippers that could hold a tank together when what we needed were plastic-toothed all-purpose zippers. These great buys took up precious space in our sewing areas for years, never earning their keep.

Treat buttons the same way as zippers; separate colors and kinds into Zip-locked bags or glass jars. Make sure you keep only what you need and like. Remember, buttons tend to look dated and shoddy in less time than other sewing notions.

Any professional seamstress will tell you that careful attention to detail is what gives a homesewn garment a professional look. Trims, such as piping, help with this look. Wrap and secure piping, lace, and other trims around small cardboard rectangles and store them in a container such as a shoebox. This eliminates messy, time-consuming tangles. You'll need a convenient place for all these notion containers, and if you don't have an accommodating sewing cabinet, you'll need a cupboard or shelved closet handy to your sewing spot.

If quilting is one of your passions, you probably have an accumulation of quilting notions, templates, and patterns. For convenience, separate these from the rest of your sewing notions and patterns. (If you have enough quilting patterns and templates, you may want to store them with your regular patterns, behind their own divider tab.) Quilting notions, such as needles, snipping scissors, rotary cutter, straightedge, thumbtacks, marking pen, clamps, and thimbles, could be stored in a labeled container such as a shoebox or drawstring bag. Alice hangs her bag of notions on an inside closet wall, alongside her various quilting frames.

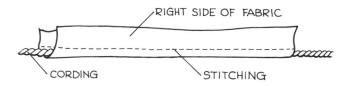

Make your own piping by cutting bias strips 1 to 1½ inches wide. With the strips wrong side up, lay the cording along the fabric's vertical length, down the middle of the bias strips. Fold the fabric in half lengthwise over the cording. (Cording can even be doubled strands of acrylic yarn.) Using a zipper foot, stitch fabric lengths, keeping the zipper foot as close to the cording as possible.

T.L.C. FOR YOUR SEWING EQUIPMENT

Sewing equipment deserves proper care and maintenance. Routine oiling (if yours is the type that needs it), dusting, cleaning, and needle-changing are the keys to keeping your machines operating properly longer. Fabric scissors need regular sharpening—and be sure to use them only on fabric. (Other family members may not respect this rule, so the scissors may be better off hidden away, out of harm's reach.) Throw away all dull and bent pins and needles—don't even save them for the bulletin board. The next time you cut out a pattern you will thank yourself.

WHAT ABOUT MENDING?

An out-of-control pile of mending constantly bidding for attention is distracting and depressing. You'd really like to cut out that new dress or start that new quilt top, but you really shouldn't until you get the mending done. Well, if you're anything like us or the thousands of home managers we've surveyed, you don't get the mending done. We all hate mending. Yet we allow it to accumulate and keep us from what we really want to do. Thus we've set up a cycle of nonproductivity—and that's where the depression enters in. Pauline says one of the most liberating and exhilarating moments in streamlining her own home came when she dumped two large packing boxes of mending into the trash and charity bags.

So to eliminate the "pending mending" annoyance, sort through and get rid of articles that no longer fit anyone or are out of style, others you don't like, and anything you have no intention of mending. (Be honest.) For example, if you don't know how to put a fly zipper in, or don't have the time or energy to mess with it, don't save pants that need this item replaced. Either have your local cleaners do it (for seven to ten dollars) or send them to charity. (When you consider the high cost of good jeans and slacks today, a seven- to ten-dollar investment isn't that big a deal.)

After this realistic streamlining, you should have whittled the mending pile down to a manageable size. You should be keeping only clothing that will be serviceable and look nice after it is repaired. Now, mend the stuff and move on to what you *really* want to do—which is probably some creative sewing or quilting.

SEW-SEW DETAILS

If your sewing area is large enough, consider storing and using the ironing board there. When it's not in use, it could be tucked away onto a door-mounted caddy.

Sewing is easier and more fun in a well-lighted, cheerful spot. A good sewing lamp is as important as a good machine, as helpful as a sharp needle. So if you don't already have good lighting, put a clamp light on your Wants list.

Last but not really least, a bulletin board hung by the sewing machine is a great place to post instructions, sewing ideas, the repair shop number, family measurements, and even your children's drawings and handiwork.

You'll find there's nothing more inviting and motivating than a streamlined, orderly sewing area—it makes you love sewing all the more.

FOURTEEN

NO MORE
NO-CAR GARAGE

Park cars, not junk, in the garage

Consider any ten homes on your block. Then ask yourself how many of the occupants can get their car into their garage. Although the original purpose of the garage is for parking your car, many people use it for indiscriminate storage, too. The garage is often treated as a warehouse; what can't fit into the house will surely fit into the garage. This results in piles of unused stuff, unwanted stuff, unneeded stuff, even lost stuff, all to be dealt with later. Only "later" never does come, and the garage gets deeper and deeper in stuff. The garage becomes so overloaded that instead of being a one- or two-car garage, it becomes a no-car garage.

Digging out a garage is easier if you do it in warm weather and allow yourself two to three days to complete the job. Employ the usual streamlining techniques and ask the key questions—Do I like it? Do I use it? Do I need it? Do I have room for it?—to decide what to keep and what to toss. When you are finished, the garage should be completely emptied and you should be dealing with only keeper piles. (Incidentally, this is an excellent time to clean and seal the garage floor. Don Aslett's *Is There Life After Housework?* has good instructions for this. He says to apply concrete sealer to any cement work, because porous concrete traps dirt and dust like a sponge and "bleeds," so after sweeping, soil is still there, looking ugly and waiting to be tracked into your house or car. Sealer eliminates the bleeding problem and makes routine cleaning, using an industrial-sized dust mop, an easy task. And while you're waiting the two days for the floor sealer to dry, you could have a garage sale—in the driveway—if that appeals to you. See tips in "Successful Garage Sales," this chapter.)

Because you don't have to be concerned with design and decor in the garage, you will be able to use walls and ceilings for hanging most things that are still stored here. But keep in mind that things stored in the garage need protection from dust and dirt. (Drawstring bags or plastic garbage sacks are great for this.)

The way to get the most out of garage space is to designate separate areas for work and activity centers, just as you did in the kitchen. Here are some typical garage centers:

A no-car garage usually stores unused, unwanted, unneeded, and even lost items.

- Car care center
- Tool and building supply center
- Yard and garden center
- Recycling center
- Activity center (bikes and outside toys such as swimming or wading pool items and sandbox toys go here)
- Barbeque center
- Camping equipment center
- Sports equipment center (for all seasons)
- Pet center (if the pet is an outdoor animal)
- Household storage center

How often you use these centers will determine where to place them in your garage. For example, if you are an avid camper but leave your car maintenance to a professional mechanic, then your camping equipment will be assigned a place for easy access and the car care center will not have priority space.

CAR CARE CENTER/
TOOL AND BUILDING SUPPLY CENTER

Consider putting car care equipment and other tools adjacent to each other for easy access. Getting as much as possible off the floor will keep you from tripping over things and enable you to keep the floor cleaner. To accomplish this, group and store like tools and supplies together; keep smaller tools and supplies that cannot be hung in drawers. Store car care equipment and supplies in the same manner. For drawers, consider using an old dresser that is no longer welcome

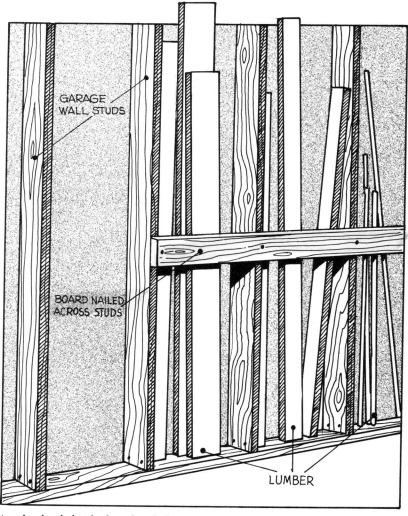

Store lumber behind a board nailed across garage-wall studs.

in the house. Building supplies such as lumber can be stored between the studs of garage walls behind a small board nailed across the studs to keep these supplies in place.

Car glove compartments, consoles, trunks and cargo areas, even "map pockets" need to be streamlined and given specific assignments to prevent overload and a trashy appearance. Our latest informal survey of minivan map pockets gave us conclusive evidence that they are used for everything *but* maps. Sticky Popsicle sticks, tattered coloring books, used facial tissues, broken pencils and dead pens are just a few of the things hiding out in what *could* be a super amenity to the family car. But without a specific assignment, the map pocket becomes the "gross pocket"!

YARD AND GARDEN CENTER

Lawn mowers, snowblowers, and Rototillers will occupy floor space. Hang shovels, rakes, trimmers, pruners, and so on from nails or on specially made tool racks, which are available in hardware stores. It's also worth investing in a garden hose rack or two. Ladders and wheelbarrows can also be hung for convenience.

> As a ladder stabilizer, a couple old pairs of tennis shoes give greater stability on soft ground; just place a shoe over each foot of the ladder.

Store all insecticides, sprays, or other chemicals in *labeled* containers or on shelves out of reach of children. Put smaller items such as garden gloves and sprinklers in a labeled container for quick retrieval. These items can also be hung up in drawstring bags.

Although logic would have you store your garden seed with the yard and garden supplies, prudence advises against it. Temperature extremes in the garage aren't good for seed; chances of germination are reduced and deterioration hastened. So keep garden seeds in labeled, airtight containers (glass canning jars are good) in your indoor storage area.

> Fine garden seed, such as carrot or spinach seed, can be mixed with sand or garden loam in the proportion of one pack of seed to four cups of sand. Put this mixture in a container with a pour spout, such as a half-gallon milk carton; shake it well to disperse the seed throughout the sand. Plant the seed by slowly pouring the mixture from the container down the garden row. Or broadcast the seed from this container onto the seed bed. The sand is an automatic thinning aid.

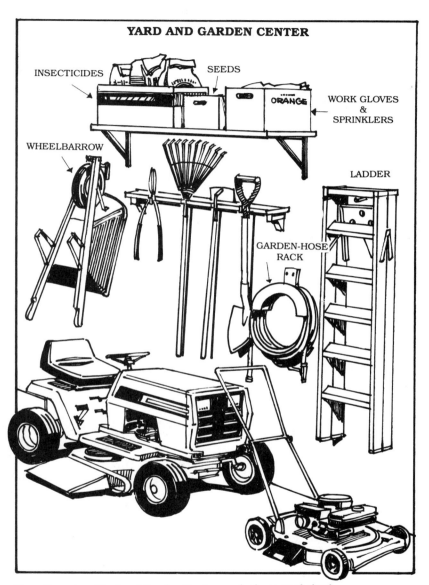

YARD AND GARDEN CENTER

INSECTICIDES

SEEDS

WORK GLOVES & SPRINKLERS

WHEELBARROW

LADDER

GARDEN-HOSE RACK

Many items in a Yard and Garden Center can be hung or shelved.

When yard and garden work is finished, avoid tracking dirt inside by assigning a place to hang outside work clothes and shoes. If you want garbage cans in the garage, get them off the floor by using a wall-hung rack or frame. Attach a chain or rope to the side supports and draw it across the front of the cans to keep them upright. Use this rack on the outside of a garage wall if you prefer.

Keep garage-stored firewood in bounds by stacking it in a rack or frame. A separate container of kindling is a time-saving convenience. In parts of the country where termites are a problem, people are strongly advised to store wood *outside* the house or garage; if you live in one of these regions, you can still keep your wood neat and fireplace-ready by storing it in a covered rack or frame.

RECYCLING CENTER

Interest in recycling is becoming increasingly widespread, and in many parts of the country trash sorting (for eventual recycling) is now mandatory. This activity creates a tremendous challenge for space and clutter control. So if sorting and/or recycling are part of your lifestyle, avoid the clutter, confusion, and eyesore this can cause by setting up your own mini-recycling center. Have a clearly labeled container for each category being saved. The containers could be metal or plastic trash cans, wooden bins, fifty-five gallon drums, even sturdy large cardboard boxes. Crushed aluminum cans, since they are lightweight,

Options for containers in a recycling center include trash bags, wooden bins, and trash cans. Keep your recycling center in the garage or storage shed.

can be saved in hanging bags, such as heavy-duty plastic trash bags, fabric drawstring bags, or even gunny sacks. Newspapers, glass, and other metal will probably need floor space, however. Visit your local recycling center on a regular basis to keep this area under control.

ACTIVITY CENTER

Outside toys need adequate storage space. Many items, such as a small wading pool, bike training wheels, or bike tire pump, can be hung. Provide shelves for toy trucks, cars, scoop shovels, and other sandbox toys. Avoid using an open box for toy storage—this invites indiscriminate tossing, chucking, and stuffing.

There are various ways to store bikes. Mountain bikes and traditional ten- or twelve-speeds can be stored on a rack made from two-by-fours notched to support cross bars. You can suspend bikes from large sturdy hooks on rafters or walls. One family we know, who must rely heavily on the garage for their total

Large hooks attached to the eaves provide an imaginative solution to bicycle storage.

Suspend a ten-speed from the rafters by large hooks.

Or create your own standup bike storage

storage needs, even stores their bikes during winter on large hooks under the eaves of their home, outside the garage and away from public view, thus freeing up precious space inside.

Another idea is to construct a wrought iron gate rack for standup bike storage. All you need to make this is a four-foot section of porch railing, plus mounting hardware and some scrap lumber. The frame is made from two-by-fours lap-jointed at the corners and screwed together. Another two-by-four joins the ends together to keep the structure rigid.

And finally, from the June 1989 issue of *Better Homes and Gardens* comes this idea: If you have the garage floor space to spare, measure off enough space to accommodate all of your child's outdoor gear—bike, scooter, Big Wheel, skateboard, roller skates, wagon, dump trucks and bull dozers, and so on; spray paint lines defining this space (perhaps a six-by-six-foot square or similarly sized rectangle, depending on the amount of gear that needs storage); and add the child's initials at the entrance. Corral and conquer seems to be the idea here, and one of its advantages is the ease with which children can get and put back their own things.

BARBEQUE CENTER

The style of your barbeque grill determines how you store it. Most grills on legs and smaller hibachis can be hung on hooks from rafters or walls. Propane grills are heavier and therefore difficult if not impossible to hang, so they require floor space. Don't overlook the possibility of grouping barbeque utensils with the grill and either storing them inside the propane kind, in a plastic bag for cleanliness, or bagging them and hanging the bag alongside the grill. Store the charcoal and starter fluid there, too.

CAMPING EQUIPMENT CENTER

If you store this equipment in the garage, then store it properly, as described in Chapter 15: Consolidate, hang as much as possible, and keep it inventoried.

Consider storing the picnic jug, picnic tablecloth, perhaps even the picnic basket inside your camper cooler. We always keep extra paper plates plus paper plate holders, cups, plastic utensils, matches, and a can opener in our picnic baskets. Some avid campers house all the cooking gear (cast iron pots, pans, griddle, utensils, dish soap, scouring pads, dish towels, dish cloths, and dish tub) in a wooden or metal box with handles, such as a footlocker.

Tent campers can keep tent pegs, poles, whisk broom, and a sheathed hatchet inside a large duffle or drawstring bag made just for this purpose. Deflated air mattresses can be folded lengthwise in thirds, rolled up into small units, and secured with elastics. These can then be stored inside a specially marked drawstring bag and kept with the sleeping bags and a small foot-type air pump. If you use foam mattresses under your sleeping bags, they can be rolled into tight cylinders, secured with cord, popped into drawstring bags, and hung up as well.

This is also the center where the tackle box, fishing poles (in a tubular container), reels, catch bag, and rubber waders would go.

We know of one camping center so efficiently set up that it has individual backpacks, always loaded and ready for travel, hung in dust covers from bike hooks along the top of a garage wall beside the shelved picnic gear.

SPORTS EQUIPMENT CENTER

Most sports equipment can be hung, so designate specific wall space for this. (Good sports equipment is expensive; use drawstring bags or plastic garbage bags to protect it from dust and dirt.) The following equipment is especially suited to being hung, either loose or in containers:

- All balls and ball-related equipment—mitts and bats, shoes, knee pads, inflating needles (in their own small pouch inside the large bag), small bicycle pump
- Swimming and pool accessories—fins, goggles, nose and earplugs (again, in their own small pouch inside the large bag), snorkles, deflated air mattresses and inner tubes, and so on, bundled in a durable drawstring bag
- Snow ski equipment—ski poles, snow boots, goggles, ski wax, ski gloves, ski hats, ski thermals (with smaller items grouped together in drawstring bags)
- Croquet sets and golf clubs, *if* you use sturdy hooks and cover the equipment with plastic bags
- Tennis rackets and badminton sets—Hang related items in labeled bags.
- Sleds and toboggans
- Bicycles
- Stilts and pogo sticks

PET CENTER

Pet food and supplies need to be stored in a place that is easy to keep clean. If your garage is attached or handy to your house, consider putting this area near the garage door so it and the pet feeding dish can be hosed down for easier maintenance. But if your garage is well removed from your home, then consider

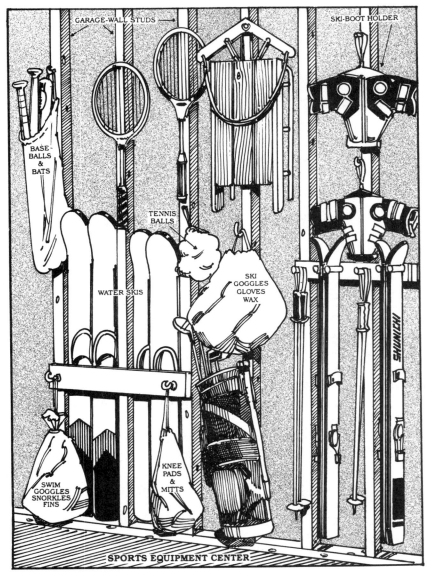

In this Sports Equipment Center, small pieces of equipment are stored in hanging drawstring bags.

setting up a feeding station inside the house but near your back door. To help avoid spilling pet food and for easier dispensing, put dry cat food into an empty gallon plastic milk jug; a milk carton works well for large-chunked dog food, too. Keep a can opener, to be used for pet food only, in the pet center, and place newspaper or a paper bag under the feeding bowls for snappy cleanup.

HOUSEHOLD STORAGE CENTER

If you lack storage space inside the house, you're probably extra appreciative of your garage space, and a household storage center is a must. Designate a specific section of your garage for storage. The luggage, card table and folding chairs, turkey roaster, boxes of Christmas decorations, boxes of empty canning jars plus the canning equipment, a case of toilet paper, extra boxes of laundry and dishwasher detergent, and so on, are things that would store well in the garage. Set this center up with durable shelving and heavy-duty hooks. Use the walls and ceiling to hang as much as possible. Protect stored items with dust covers. Be sure to group like categories together and to label containers for easy recognition of contents.

If you're a book/magazine storer, then at least once a year it is wise to make yourself dig into them, asking all the key questions. Remember, they are taking up valuable space that is most likely needed for other things.

Here are a couple of "ultimates" in the way of household garage storage that we've seen: One family partitioned off a six-by-thirteen-foot section, insulated it, installed a light, and equipped it with floor-to-ceiling shelves running down both thirteen-foot walls. With only a thirty-inch walkway between shelved walls, you can imagine how much this partitioned area stores. Another family dedicated one entire garage wall (from floor to ceiling) to recycled closets and cupboards. All doors can be locked and all closet/cupboard inside walls are lined with pegboard. The advantages of both systems are that the garage appears neater, the stored items are better protected, and the enclosed spaces discourage random drop-offs (so things tend to be put back where they belong and spaces can fulfill their specific assignments).

A WORD TO THE WISE

Be on your guard when dealing with garage contents and centers. There is no other area of your home or property that becomes as overloaded and discombobulated as the garage—simply because it's such a handy, wide open, usually ugly space. This is where we are sorely tempted to commit the sin of putting things "just for now." Be aware, then, that because of the wide variety of things stored there, plus the reasons mentioned above, you will need to streamline and reassign stuff on a regular basis—probably quarterly.

SUCCESSFUL GARAGE SALES

A garage sale—also known as a tag, yard, or barn sale—is a terrific way to dispose of things no longer needed, especially since the money you make is virtually all profit. If you plan ahead and use these tips (shared by the Associated Press in our local newspaper), yours will be a successful garage sale:

- Choose a time of year when the weather is likely to cooperate and plan to hold the sale on a weekend when people are home (the July 4th weekend may not be the best choice).
- About a month before the sale, check with your local government offices to see whether a special permit is required and whether you must collect sales taxes.
- Assemble items to be sold. If you don't have enough, ask friends to participate in the sale.
- Run an ad in your local newspaper giving the location of the sale, the date, and the hours. Include the merchandise range.
- Your advertising signs should be large, with bold and easy-to-read lettering. Put them along the most travelled roads near the sale location, and on poles and trees at intersections. Also put them at supermarkets, bus stops, and social centers. Wherever you post signs, make sure it's legal to do so. Keep a record of where these signs are so you can take them down after the sale is over.
- Price goods with removable tags. Use different colors or initials for different owners. Generally, you will price goods from 10 to 50 percent of what it would cost new, depending on age and condition. When in doubt, price lower. After all—your garage sale items are all the things you no longer like, use, need, want, or have room for. You may as well have someone else *pay you* to haul them away—even if the pay is lower than you originally anticipated. In many cases, you can determine the approximate value of merchandise by consulting the current edition of one of the large mail order catalogs.
- On sale day, arrange your things on nicely covered, amply-sized tables. Visual attractiveness and the orderly display of things counts—it's called "curb appeal"—and it can go a long way toward psychologically selling customers. So group like items together (but not too tightly): clothes on racks (be sure to indicate the size if it is not on a garment label); books on shelves; and so on. Plug in an extension cord for testing appliances and other electrical items. And be sure to have a "Plan B" in case of rain.
- Finally, start with forty to fifty dollars in small bills and change. Keep your money in a cash box with the lid closed when not in use. Designate one person as the cashier, seated at the exit end of the flow of traffic.

ANOTHER CATCHALL: THE BACK PORCH OR DECK

While these areas may not be a part of the garage, they do suffer from some of the same maladies. Thus, we felt it proper to treat this subject here.

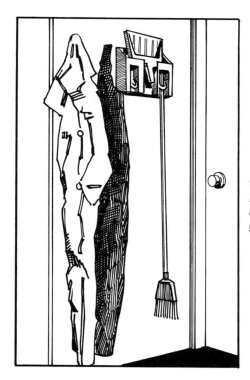

Take advantage of space in an enclosed back porch or deck to hang your broom, dustpan, and perhaps your yard and garden clothes.

You know the typical back porch or deck — no matter what the size or shape, they have a few things in common. They're adjacent to an entrance and are an informal introduction to the house. They're part of a traffic pattern, often a busy one. They're often dirty and hard to keep clean. They tend to be catchalls. Frequently, they're cluttered with unrelated items. Little or no thought is given to their arrangement, function, or purpose. They're often unattractive. They can be embarrassing, irritating, and bothersome.

All the same, another outside entrance to the house is a valuable amenity. It's worth having, so don't try to ignore it — instead, fix it up.

An ideal back porch or deck is functional, clean, and easy to keep that way. Whether yours consists of no more than cement steps or a cement slab, or is more elaborate — say, a glassed-in room or a wooden deck — achieving the ideal is possible.

First, carefully assess what you have to work with. Here are some ideas that will help you transform the bothersome into the ideal:

- Seal concrete. Then consider purchasing industrial quality doormats. They're the ultimate answer to eliminating much of the tracked-in grit and grime. Janitorial supply houses offer various colors and sizes.

- Hang as much as possible. (If you have a closed-in back porch or deck, this could be the spot to hang the broom, mop, dustpan, a paper bag holder, your yard and garden clothes, maybe even the flyswatter.) The wall along a deck is usually the back of the house. This could support a few hanging things, such as a drawstring bag containing the barbeque utensils (if these things cannot go in a garage). If you are handy, you might consider building a built-in bench with hinged seat to be used as an out-of-sight storage area for barbeque utensils and so on.

- Don't allow this area to be used as an annex to the garage. Yard and garden tools often end up on the back porch or deck because people don't take the time to put them away. Someone gasses up the lawn mower, sets the gas can on the back porch, and there it stays. If you have no garage, don't allow this area to look like a makeshift garage. There is *always* another place for things, even if it's a metal shed, old school lockers, a large wooden box, and so on. (If there isn't a proper place for something, create one. If you can't, the something probably ought to go.)

- Make the back porch or deck a pleasant place to spend time. Consider putting potted plants, comfortable lawn furniture, a picnic table, hammock, or whatever suits your fancy (and your space) out there. If your family likes to barbeque, perhaps you'd like to build a fire pit in the backyard. (For complete how-to instructions, see the Back-of-the-Book Bonuses section.)

- If there's no other place to store your lawn furniture during the off season, then perhaps the wooden deck will be your spot. If it's foldable furniture, consider covering it with large plastic trash bags and hanging it where you can (on the back of the house, which would be one side of the deck, for example).

FIFTEEN

THE SUPER STORAGE AREA

Managing crawl spaces, basements and other storage areas

When we discuss "storage area," we're referring to any spot that you've dedicated specifically to *storage*. This could be the attic, part of the basement, a section of the garage, a large closet (or several closets), a backyard shed, or even an away-from-home rental unit.

Actually, the kind of storage area we're talking about in this chapter should not be a "someplace else," but it is too often treated as if it were. When we can't decide where something goes, we just put it someplace, and that someplace is the storage area. And several years of shoving storage is bad news, for you and the storage.

When it comes to overload, the storage area is usually one of the worst cases. If you've ever been even an occasional storage-shover, then you probably don't know for sure what's in there or where anything is. Wasted space, often caused by saving duplicates, is another problem the average storage area faces. These often include old looseleaf binders, bathroom hardware, toilet tank lids, broken TVs, warped record albums, orphaned appliance cords, old wire refrigerator shelves, spare dining room chair seats, the flat spare tire for the Volkswagen Bug that was sold eight years ago, and so on.

This area is probably entombing some dead storage, too. Dead storage is what has been forgotten, untouched, unused, unopened. We know many home managers who have boxes in their storage area that once filled have never been reopened—they stay sealed from move to move. One typical dead storage item is hand-me-down clothes. We store and store them but seldom wear them; they get buried and forgotten. When they're finally discovered, everyone has outgrown them, or the stuff is so totally out of style that no one would be caught dead in them. Everything in storage should be "alive," waiting to go into service; rather than "dead" and hiding out from the garbage or local charity.

Alive and not dead, efficient and not full—that's a professional storage area. And an efficient and professional storage area is a key part of the skeleton of your home. Just as a warehouse is the backbone of any successfully operated business or industry, the storage area is the backbone to your home. Overload it and the whole house suffers. An efficient and professional storage area is also the backup system for the entire home. A home backup system anticipates needs and is prepared to meet them. For instance, we eventually run out of toilet paper, plastic wrap, toothpaste, cellophane tape, dishwasher detergent, and so on. We periodically need to replace lightbulbs, vacuum belts and bags, furnace filters, car oil, and so on. A backup system holds replacements for all these items.

A good storage area is also a holding spot for all temporarily inactive keepers. For instance, although you may not need them now, if another baby is in your plans, you will eventually need the crib bumpers, bassinet, and high chair put back in service. The same goes for good hand-me-downs. Suitcases are another "temporarily inactive" group.

This holding area keeps temporarily inactive items out of the active main flow of the home. It provides orderly, efficient protection for things that are waiting for their term of service.

Deal with this spot as you did the kitchen and garage, emptying it completely and putting the contents in related piles. Streamline these piles until only keepers are left. Then designate centers in your storage area according to available space and keeper categories. Your categories of keeper piles automatically determine your centers.

Basically, there are two types of storage: seasonal-occasional and home management. Seasonal-occasional storage is just what the name implies— things kept here are *used* only seasonally or occasionally. These things aren't used often enough to merit prime space in the rest of the home, so they're assigned to the storage area. Some possible examples: home canning equipment, sports equipment, holiday decorations, summer wear and beach towels, picnic and camping supplies, suitcases, turkey roaster, good hand-me-downs, quilting frames and stands (if there's no room in your sewing area), and so on. Home management storage items, again, are what the name implies—backup supplies of anything *used* in managing a home (toilet paper, dish, bath, and laundry soaps, grooming and hygiene products, plastic wrap, tin foil, paper towels, light bulbs, and so on).

One storage area can efficiently house both types if you designate specific centers. If you have loads of storage space, you could split the two categories up, sending one type to one area and the other type to another area. However you do it, the point is to carefully assess all intended storage items, evaluate and assign specific spots to each storage category, and group and store like items together.

Notice how supermarkets group and store like items together, using as much vertical space as possible, often stacking from the floor to the ceiling.

This type of storage uses space efficiently, and it adapts well to home storage areas.

SEASONAL-OCCASIONAL STORAGE

The garage, basement, crawl space, attic, and shed are obvious places for this type of storage. What if you don't have space like that available? You could convert a typical linen closet (see the "No-Linen-Closetology" section in Chapter 11) into a storage area, or install floor to ceiling shelves in a portion of a clothes closet. If possible, avoid under-the-bed storage, however. (See "Under the Bed" in Chapter 4.)

There are some things you can do to maximize your space and increase your storing efficiency. Use all available space within the area by hanging as much as possible. For example, bag and hang spare bath and bed linens; do the same for sleeping bags and extra toys. Almost anything with a handle or a hole in it can be hung: turkey roaster (with the baster inside), Christmas tree stand, Christmas tree decorations (in drawstring bags), Halloween costumes (again, in drawstring bags), high chair, even the card table and folding chairs. (You may want to tie a rope through some of these handles or holes for easier hanging.)

Consolidation is another space saver. Many suitcase sets can be packed inside one another: the tote or carry-on bag inside the small case, and then the small case inside the large. The bassinet could hold a drawstring bag or box of baby clothes or bedding, baby room decor items, or perhaps a bag of baby toys. Then, of course, hang these groups of consolidated items up.

Be creative with your shelving. Besides the assembled metal shelves and traditional wooden shelves, you can use boards laid across cement blocks (solid pine is better than pressed board since pressed board bends easily under weight) or boards laid across storage buckets, ceramic pipe, bricks—even gallon jars filled with beans, wheat, rice, popcorn, and so on can support shelf boards.

To maintain control of this area, always consider how any given item is used, where it is used, and how often it's used—then put things where they belong. We once worked with a man who owned a few rental units; his home storage area was littered with old toilet seats and plumbing fixtures. Since he was sure he'd need these things as replacements, it made good sense to him to keep them, but we suggested this collection be stored at the rental units, thus freeing up valuable space and giving him more control of his home storage area.

HOME MANAGEMENT STORAGE

The garage is an adequate place for this, but it has its drawbacks: It gets dirty easily and is hard to clean, and it is subject to temperature extremes that shorten shelf life for perishables such as canned goods and garden seeds. Even more than household storage, garage storage calls for careful packaging and pestproof containers. Sometimes the garage is inconveniently located. Remember, too, that cement floors sweat, causing metal containers to rust and paper and cardboard to deteriorate. That means you'll need to lay down wooden slats or skids before you stack containers on the floor. Skids, more commonly known as wooden pallets, are often used in industry and are frequently available for free (just watch along roadsides as you drive; they're often piled in lots adjacent to industrial sites and have a sign posted nearby that says "free wood"). Should you decide to purchase wooden slats, be sure to have your lumberyard cut them to your specifications (two-by-fours work best).

The garage is better than nothing, though, and you can improve a garage storage situation by framing a portion in, sheetrocking, and insulating it, thereby creating a mini storage area. (See Chapter 14, the "Household Storage Center" section, for more on this.)

The crawl space beneath the house will also work, even if the floor is dirt, although you'll need to use wooden slats or skids here, too. We've seen some very ingenious ideas applied to the crawl space, from short shelving to floor-joist hanging. Many things can be put in drawstring bags and hung from the floor joists. It's not necessary to give shelf space to items such as first-aid supplies, garden seeds, candles, matches, grooming and hygiene products, sewing notions, light bulbs, and so on. Even five-gallon buckets or plastic gallon milk jugs (filled with water, pet food, bulk detergent, and so on) can be hung if the nails are big enough, hammered in far enough, and put in at a severe angle. And you'll find one of the pluses to storing in a crawl space is the fairly constant temperature factor.

Your overhead crawl space, the attic, will work as well, only in this case you'll be hanging things from roof trusses or rafters. The major drawback here, as in the garage, is the temperature extremes. Also, it may not be easily accessible or safe – can you imagine climbing a pull-down ladder with your arms full of stuff? But again, it *is* better than nothing.

Although it's true that storage isn't used as much if it's hard to get to, it's also true that you'll be more inclined to use it if it is stocked in an efficient, orderly way. With thoughtful planning, even attic or crawl space storage can be put to work.

Another good storage spot is the hall linen closet. Empty it out completely and assign specific categories of storage to each shelf. (For more on this idea, see Chapter 11, "More No-Linen-Closetology.")

We can't overlook the basement as a natural storage center. Whether you use just a section of it or devote the entire area to storage, be sure to have a specific plan for placing your categories of things – don't just cram and stuff things here and there. You may want to draw up a floor plan on graph paper, labeling each area. (Keep this floor plan with your "finger-tip" storage cards, described in Chapter 3.) Seal concrete floors before laying down wooden slats for your stacking.

BASIC STORAGE TIPS

Here are some tips for stocking and maintaining a storage area so it will be a living asset to your home rather than a graveyard for dead stuff.

- Again, group and store like items together, just as the grocery store does; don't scatter.
- Consolidate as much as possible.

> To transfer dry items such as bulk detergent or pet food into other containers, cut the bottom off a large paper grocery sack. Then insert it into the mouth of a gallon jar or other small-mouthed container. Spread it apart at the bottom, fan it out at the top, and use it as a giant funnel.

- Hang as much as possible.
- Use the grocery store arrangement by lining the perimeter of your area with shelving, then run stacks of shelves both parallel and perpendicular to this. Though intended for an actual storage room, this arrangement also works in a crawl space.
- Assign a specific space for empties. No more setting empty jars, buckets, or drawstring bags on a shelf in front of full containers.
- For home management and backup storage in particular, you will want to use a perpetual inventory system: Keep an accurate record of things on an inventory sheet using these headings: What (or Item), Amount, and Location. Other pertinent headings are Date of Purchase, Date Opened, and Expiration Date. See pages 156 and 157 for examples. The best way to keep track of this information is to log it onto pages with the aforementioned headings, keep these pages in a three-ring binder, and keep the binder either in your storage area or with your office center (See the "Office Center" section in Chapter 10).
  The need for inventorying is one of the main reasons for making your storage convenient. If you can't get to it, you won't rotate or inventory it.
- Store home management and backup supplies that your family uses and

HOME MANAGEMENT STORAGE

Item	Amount	Date Purchased	Location
Toilet paper	4 four packs (16 rolls)	9/18/91	under basement stairs

BACKUP STORAGE

Item	Amount	Date Purchased	Expiration Date	Location
1 case tuna	48 cans	4/20/91	12/93	hall closet

likes, and use what you store. Alice found a fantastic buy on an off-brand of toothpaste, so she bought twelve tubes. No wonder it was such a great buy—it tasted like white glue. Her family detested it and refused to use it. So her wonderful bargain sat ("No returns on SALE items, thank you"), taking up precious space. She finally chucked it. She discovered that the biggest expense was not in the money she paid for the junk, but in the space she wasted to store it.

Don't be tempted to just shove things into the storage area until you can find another place for them. Get into the habit of practicing on-the-spot assessment by making immediate decisions. The warning we issued in Chapter 14 applies here, also: Because storage areas are often wide open spaces and there's such a great variety of things stored there, you will need to streamline and perhaps reassign items on a regular basis—perhaps quarterly. The bottom line? Keep the "backbone" of your household skeleton lightly and efficiently loaded, and you'll experience greater efficiency and control throughout the rest of your home.

Finally, an efficient, convenient, well-stocked storage area can mean the difference between just getting by and enjoying comfort and your usual standard of living indefinitely. It is also a great hedge against inflation and a source of peace of mind. It's not just a "someplace else."

IT REALLY *IS* HERE
. . . SOMEWHERE

The beginning of a more orderly lifestyle

I t really is here . . . somewhere! Not only the end of the book, but the beginning of an improved lifestyle. No more creeping clutter; no more bulging closets, cupboards, and drawers; no more time wasted doing the household shuffle. No more excuses; no more frustration. Now *you* are in control, truly a professional home manager.

As you're enjoying this constant order and control, remember one thing: Bad habits die hard. Because they're tough to kill, you must be even tougher in your resolve to establish good ones. Remember what author and home efficiency expert Bonnie McCullough says: "People are more important than things, but the *order* of things affects people." So don't give in to the old ways of managing (or mismanaging) your home; stick with your streamlining as a lifestyle. And don't let a little backsliding by you or others discourage you. It'll happen once in a while, but it's nothing to panic over, because you can recapture control and order as quickly as it was lost.

As we travel across the country with our Clutter Therapy consulting and seminars, we find over and over again that few people have things exactly the way they'd like them. Almost everyone has plenty to whine and complain about, plenty to feel sorry for themselves over. When the temptation to slip into this style of "coping" arises, it's helpful to remember John R. Noe's wise perspective from his book *Peak Performance Principles for High Achievers*. He says, "We cannot control what happens to us, or what people do to us, or where we start in the race of life. But we *can* control how we react to our experiences. We can allow circumstances to bury us, or we can choose to rise above them and become high achievers." It's been shown that success in anything, including home managing, is a combination of having the right attitudes, the right principles, the right strategies, and the right techniques, and then being willing to pay the price to implement them. In order to have long-term control over your physical spaces and things, you must be willing to trade old ways of thinking and functioning for new concepts and approaches. You'll also need to expend some time and energy initially to put a new system in place. But we believe that if you want to change your lot in life, you must first start with the little lot you're living on. In this book we've provided the principles, strategies, and techniques that, coupled with your desire for change and willingness to pay the price, virtually guarantee your success as a high achiever in managing your home. Thus our twofold wish for you: May you continue to rise above your circumstances, and may your household shovel always be full!

BACK-OF-THE-BOOK BONUSES

HOOK IT
(Using standard screw-in hooks, nails, eyebolts)

THE MANY LIVES
OF A DRAWSTRING BAG

HOW TO MAKE
DRAWSTRING BAGS —
THE STREAMLINED WAY

HOW TO MAKE
A CLOSET LAUNDRY BAG

HOW TO BUILD A FIRE PIT

HOOK IT

(Using standard screw-in hooks, nails, eyebolts)

AREA	WHERE	WHAT
Kitchen	behind refrigerator or underneath an above-the-refrigerator cupboard	broom, dustpan, mop, whisk broom
	underside of countertops (at end of bank of cupboards)	phone book, calendar
	on inside of cupboard doors and walls; underside of cupboard shelves	large plastic bowl, colander, dish drainer tray (with hole in one end and string tied through for loop), turkey roaster, pots and pans, utensils, appliance cords (wound and secured), measuring cups, grater, bag and wrap holder, cleaning supplies holder, trash holder
Bedroom	wooden hangers (to be hung in closet)	belts, scarves, hair ribbons, necklaces
Bathroom	end of plunger handle and the underside of vanity top	plunger
Garage or Outside Storage Shed	walls/studs; ceiling joists; undersides of shelves	bikes, barbeque grills, stroller, car seat, ladders, wheelbarrow, garden tools, fertilizer spreader, yard equipment, camping equipment, kiddie wading pool, lawn chairs, spare carpet rolls, hibachi, spare tires/snow tires, hand tools, suitcases, saddles and bridles

NOTE: Certain items will store better and be easier to maintain if slipped into a large plastic bag (such as a trash bag) before hanging.

THE MANY LIVES OF A DRAWSTRING BAG

AREA	WHERE	WHAT
Kitchen	inside cupboard doors; inside cupboard walls; underneath cupboard shelves; underneath sink from underside of kitchen countertop	dry packaged mixes, extension and appliance cords, cleaning supplies and equipment, matches, lamp wicks, candles, cookie cutters, birthday cake candles and cake decorations, tool kit, shoeshine kit, pastas, dry beans, and seeds
Bathroom	inside vanity doors; underneath sink, along inside vanity walls; underneath sink from underside of vanity top; inside cupboard doors and walls	curlers, curling irons, blow dryers and attachments, hair clippers and attachments, makeup, feminine hygiene needs, bar soaps, other toiletries, extra towel set
Bedrooms	in closets along perimeter walls and underside of closet shelf; from closet ceiling; along a "hook board" on wall	toys, games, shoes, boots, sleeping bags, belts, extra bed linens, child's "treasure collection," scarves, jewelry, makeup, purses (for dust protection)
Closets	on back side of hinged door; along inside walls; from underneath closet shelf; from closet ceiling; from closet rod	seasonal sporting goods (ski accessories, soccer equipment), cold weather outerwear (hats, mittens, gloves, boots), shoeshine kits, cleaning supplies/tools, film and cameras, medicines, school supplies, sewing notions, lightbulbs, oil and acrylic paint tubes with brushes, extra toys, spare bed and bath linens
Storage	from ceiling; from underside of shelves; from back of solid doors; from ceiling or floor joists (in the case of crawl space); along walls	candles/matches/lamp wicks, seasonal items (holiday decorations), sewing notions, fabric, infant seat (for dust protection), flavorings, herbs, spices, bar soaps, toiletries (disposable razors, toothbrushes, toothpaste), school supplies, canning booklets/equipment
Garage	ceiling joists; wall studs; from underside of shelves	camping equipment, sports equipment, seasonal items (barbeque utensils, yard toys), pet supplies, garden seeds, small garden tools and gloves, sleeping bags

HOW TO MAKE DRAWSTRING BAGS — THE STREAMLINED WAY

The purpose of the bag determines your choice of fabric.

The purpose of the bag determines its width and length.

The type of drawstring used determines the casing width.

Drawstring suggestions: shoelaces, bias tape, heavy string, jute, macramé cord, chalk line, old drapery cording.

Allow ½" sems.

To "mass produce" drawstring bags:

1. Sew a tube, right sides together, the width of the finished bag plus seam allowance, and the length equaling the number of bags times their length plus the bottom seam allowances.

   Width equation: bag wide = ½" seam allowance

   Length equation: (number of bags × bag length) + (number of bags × seam allowance)

   Example: 4 bags, 12" wide, 14" long

   width = 12" + ½" = 12½" wide

   length = (4 bags × 14") + (4 bags × ½") = (56")
   + (2") = 58" long

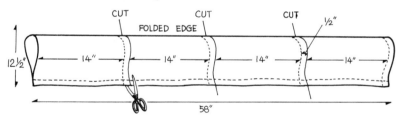

2. Stitch across the width of the tube at intervals equaling the desired bag length.
3. Cut across the tube ½" from each line of stitches.
4. Measure drawstrings for each bag. Each string should measure twice the bag width plus two inches. Example: (12" × 2) + 2" = 24" + 2" = 26" of string per bag.
5. Fasten each string into an approximate 24" loop, using an overhand knot.
6. Put the bag, still right sides together, up through this looped string.

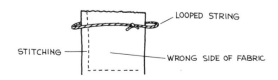

7. Fold the raw edge down over the drawstring, making the casing wide enough to allow stitching in place without catching the cord.

8. Cut small slits in the casing on each side of bag to allow the drawstring to be pulled through.

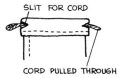

9. Finally, turn the bag right side out and pull up the drawstrings.

HOW TO MAKE A CLOSET LAUNDRY BAG

Use a sturdy wooden hanger. Its width will determine the width of the finished bag. The length of the finished bag is up to you.

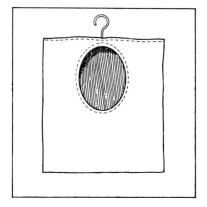

Instructions:

1. Measure two pieces of fabric of the desired width and length.

2. In one piece, cut a large circular or oval opening. Finish and reinforce this opening with bias tape.

3. Place the right sides of both pieces together and sew side, bottom, and top seams, leaving a small opening in the middle of the top seam to allow the hanger to slip through.

4. Turn the bag right-side out and insert the hanger through the opening. (It can be removed when you launder the bag.)

Note: A pillowcase works well for this project, also. Cut the circle in one side, finishing with bias tape. Stitch along the opening of the case, leaving a space for the hanger insertion.

HOW TO BUILD A FIRE PIT

A backyard fire pit is a great place for family fun and informal get-togethers – roasting hot dogs, summer night singalongs, and so on. A grill can be put across the hole for barbequing, and three Dutch ovens will fit into the pit for delicious Dutch oven meals. If you'd like to try your hand at building a brick fire pit, here's how:

Needed: Approximately 43 firebricks/shovel/hand trowel

1. Dig a straight-sided hole approximately three feet in diameter. The length of your firebrick determines the depth of the hole.

2. Line the side walls of the pit with bricks placed on end, packing soil tightly around each brick to secure it in place. The tops of the vertical bricks should sit flush with the grass around the top of the hole.

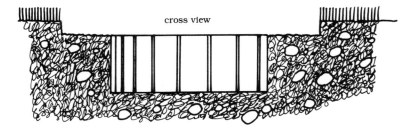

3. Cut a strip of soil and grass as wide as the length of firebricks, away from mouth of pit:

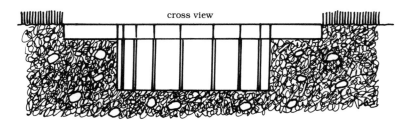

4. Lay firebricks flat in the cut-away area, fairly close together, around the mouth of the pit, so that the ends of the bricks facing the interior of the pit are on top of the ends of the vertical lining bricks. Pack tightly with soil. Grass will grow back quickly, fill in the spaces, and hold the bricks in place. (Bricks should be flush with or slightly below grass line to allow for easy mowing.)

5. Do not line the bottom of pit with bricks; leave the soil floor to permit sufficient drainage.

SUGGESTED READING:
More books to help you.

Aslett, Don. *Clutter's Last Stand.* Cincinnati: Writer's Digest Books, 1984. Using anecdotes, cartoons, quizzes, and "bumper snickers," Aslett shows how to uncover junk areas (from the basement to food), judge junk, and decide what we really *should* keep.

Aslett, Don. *Is There Life After Housework?* Cincinnati: Writer's Digest Books, 1985. Aslett shows how to save up to 75 percent of the time you spend housecleaning by using the tools and techniques of professional cleaners. Includes charts, diagrams, and step-by-step instructions for cleaning windows, carpets, furniture, and more.

Dorff, Pat. *File . . . Don't Pile.* New York: St. Martin's Press, 1983. Pat Dorff is a professional librarian, lecturer, and consultant, as well as the creator of the "File . . . Don't Pile" workshop. Her unique filing system is now available in book form.

Feldon, Leah. *Dressing Rich.* New York: G. P. Putnam's Sons, 1982. Leah Feldon outlines a practical approach to building a classical yet multipurpose wardrobe on a slim budget. Before-and-after case studies, do's and don'ts, and superior drawings make this book an absorbing resource on upgrading your wardrobe and image.

Fjelstul, Alice Bancroft, Patricia Shad, and Barbara Marhoefer. *Early American Wall Stencils in Color.* New York: E. P. Dutton, 1982. Featured are step-by-step directions for stenciling walls and fabrics, as well as more than seventy-five full-sized stencil patterns. In our opinion, this is the last word on the subject!

McCullough, Bonnie. *Bonnie's Household Organizer.* New York: St. Martin's Press, 1980. This book won't make you rich, and it won't make your work go away. What it will do, if you have a desire to improve your efficiency, is help you get organized so that you can get done what needs to be done and go on to other things.

McCullough, Bonnie, and Susan Monson. *401 Ways to Get Your Kids to Work at Home.* New York: St. Martin's Press, 1982. This book has the answers and ideas to the age-old problem of getting children to be more responsible and help more with family living. This book is a fantastic companion volume to *It's Here . . . Somewhere!*

Stoddard, Alexandra. *Living a Beautiful Life.* New York: Random House, 1986. A guide to gracious living from one of America's top interior designers, this book makes you a believer and shows you how to live the kind of life that many of us thought was only for the rich and famous. Truly inspiring reading!

Index

Activity center, garage, 143-144
Apartment box, 118
Assess, 3, 19-20, 158
   three price tags, 13
Attitudes can handicap, 28

Baby's room, 55-59
   avoid the warehouse look, 57
   closet and dresser, 55-56
   decor, 57, 58
   mom-on-the-run, 58-59
   shared rooms, 57
   toys, 55, 57
Back-of-the-book bonuses, 161-167
   drawstring bag uses and
     construction, 163-165
   fire-pit how-to's, 166-167
   hook uses, 162
   laundry bag construction, 165
Back porch or deck, 148-150
Back-to-back furniture arrangement,
   77
Baking center, 99, 106, 107
Barbeque center, garage, 144
Bathroom cleaning, 52-54
Bathroom streamlining, 46-54
   bath toys, 51
   dirty laundry, 51
   first aid supplies, 52
   guest bath, suggestions for, 52
   no storage, 50-51
   scale, tips for storing, 52
   storage ideas, 49-51
   vanity, 47-49
Benefits of streamlining, 4-11
   better looking home, 5, 10
   easier maintenance, 4, 9
   less stress, 5, 11
   more efficient layout, 4, 10
   more space, 4, 7-8
   more time and energy, 4, 5-7
   no more clutter, 4, 8-9
   peace of mind, 5, 10
Better looking home, benefit of
   streamlining, 5, 10

Bike storage, 143-144
Board games, 65, 86
Book streamlining, 63, 65, 88
Boot storage, 38
Broom and dustpan storage, 117-
   118

Cabinets, closets, and cupboards,
   119-126
   board games, 65, 86, 120
   china cabinets and built-ins, 125-
     126
   frequently used items, 122
   gift-giving tip, 120
   hall closets, 120-122
   hang it, 48, 49, 97, 98, 107, 122
   Must Return basket or box, 120-
     121
   no-linen closetology, 122-125
   seasonal things, 21, 99, 152, 153
Camping equipment center, garage,
   144-145
Car care center, garage, 139-140
Car storage areas, within, 140
Categorize physical possessions, 21
Cedar chest streamlining, 44
Charity bag
   as streamlining container, 17-18
   in laundry area, 63, 128-129
Children's clothes, 62-63
   hand-me-downs, rules for
     managing, 62-63
Cleaning products, 108
Cleanup center, 107-111
Clockwise pattern, 16, 19, 61
Closet cleaning technique, 36-40
Closet streamlining, 35-40
Clothes streamlining, adult, 35-40
   nylons, folding, 40-41
   seasonal, 39
   shoes and boots, 37-39
   slips, 40, 41
Clothing decisions, 36
Clothing, fads, 39
Clothing, never-wear, 6, 36

Clutter, 1-2, 10
no more, benefit of streamlining, 4,
8-9
visual, 24, 43
Collections, 71-72
Containers, 16, 17-19, 41, 107
Control of spaces, 4, 9, 11, 12-16
Cookbooks and recipes, 117
Cookie dough, frozen, 107
Cooking center, 95-99

Decision making, 10, 36
Don'ts, when streamlining, 25-26
Drawstring bags, 49, 66, 163-165
Dresser streamlining, 40-42, 55-56

Easier household maintenance,
benefit of streamlining, 4, 9
Efficient layout, benefit of
streamlining, 4, 10
Eight steps to control, 15-24
Empty space(s) 3, 4, 16, 24, 26
walls, 43
Energy, more, benefit of
streamlining, 4, 5-7, 22
Enforcing the changes, 30, 69, 122
Evaluate, 3, 86
and assign, 16, 19-20, 26
basic questions, 16, 19-21, 35

Fads in clothing, 39
Family room, 85-89
activity centers, 85-88
book streamlining, 88
decor, 85, 88-89
furnishings, 85
purpose(s) of, 85
Firewood, 142
Floor plans, kitchen, 99, 100-103
Furniture
arrangements, 77
family room, 85
living room, 77
overload, 72, 144
sources, 79
wall decor, using in, 78

Gantt Bar Chart, 79, 82-83

Garage, 137-150
activity center, 143-144
barbeque center, 144
bike storage, 143-144
camping equipment center, 144-
145
car care/tools and building supply
center, 139-140
car storage areas, 140
firewood, 142
ladder stabilizer, 140
pet center, 145-146
recycling center, 142-143
sales, 147-148
sports equipment center, 145
storage center, 147
streamlining, when and how to,
137-138
yard and garden center, 140-141
Garden seed, tip for planting, 140
Gift-giving
suggestions for, 67-69
time- and money-saving tip for,
120, 125
to teens, 68
younger children, 68-69
"Gravels," 98
Group and store like items together,
8, 16, 21-22, 47-48, 56, 120, 152

Hall closets, 120-122
Hand-me-down clothing, rules for
managing, 62-63
"Home managing hope," 7, 128
Household shuffle, 2, 4, 14
Household skeleton, 119, 126

Information center, 91, 112-115
Ironing board cover, how to make,
130

Junk mail, 116

Keeper, 1, 3, 4, 21
Kids' rooms, 60-69
clothing, 62-63
decor, 61
dresser, 63

enforcing the lifestyle, 30, 69, 122
gift ideas, 67-69
hand-me-down clothes, rules for
    managing, 62-63
toys, books, games, etc., 63-66
walls, 66-67
Kinder Locs, 49, 94
Kitchen, streamlining, 19, 90-118
    apartment box, 118
    baking center, 99, 106, 107
    bowls, 117, 118
    broom and dustpan, 117-118
    center locations and inventory
        chart, 91, 104-105
    cleaning products, 108
    cleanup center, 107-111
    cookbooks and recipes, 117
    cookie dough, frozen, 107
    cooking center, 95-99
    empty countertops for easier
        maintenance, 9, 90, 116-117
    floor plans, 99, 100-103
    four steps, 91-92
    "gravels," 98
    information center, 91, 112-115
    junk mail, 116
    knives and cutting tools, 117
    leftovers, 116-118
    lunch or sandwich center, 112
    microwave center, 111-112
    office center, 115-116
    onions, how to chop, 96
    pantry or food center, 111
    phone book hang-up, 114
    seasonal cooking utensils, 99
    simplicity, aim for, 93
    spaghetti bag, 96
    tableware center, 93-94
    toaster, what to do with, 112
    To Do file folder, 115
    under-the-cupboard appliances,
        97-98
    utensils, 94, 96, 97, 116, 117, 118
    walls, 91, 118

Laundry area, 127-131
    ammonia water spray, 129
    charity bag, 63, 128-129
    clear vinegar, 129
    dirty laundry, 51
    eliminate loads, 6, 49-50
    ironing board cover, how to make,
        130
    labeled laundry tubs, 131
    sock tips, 130
Laundry bag to hang, 51
Law of household ecology, 12-13, 24,
    26, 63
Law of household physics, 12-13, 21,
    24, 26, 49
Law of reduction, 13
Leftovers, kitchen, 116-118
    broom and dustpan, 117-118
    cookbooks and recipes, 117
    cutting utensils, 117
    general utensils, 116, 118
    refrigerator keepers, 117, 118
Less stress, benefit of streamlining, 5
Living room, 70-84
    collections, 71-72
    decorating, 74-76
    furnishings and accessories, 72
    furniture arranging, 77
    Gantt Bar Chart, 79, 82-83
    knickknack clutter, 71
    paper clutter, 71
    Project and Dreams Worksheet,
        79, 80-81
    purpose(s), 70
    upgrading, 84
    walls, 72-74
Lunch or sandwich center, 112

Mail, junk, 116
Maintenance, easier, benefit of
    streamlining, 4, 9
Management of things, 9
Master bedroom, 34-45
    cedar chests, 44
    closet, 35-40
    dresser, 40-42
    night stands, 43
    starting here, reason for, 34-35
    under the bed, 42-43
    walls, 43
Memory box, *see* Treasure box

Microwave center, 111-112
Mom-on-the-run, 58-59

Night stands, 43
"No-linen closetology," 122-125
  freed space, suggestions for using,
    123-125
  linens
    bath, 49-50
    bed, 123

Office center, 115-116
Onions, how to chop, 96
Organization, 3, 4
Overload, 1, 4, 5, 13, 21, 44, 90
Ownership ambiguity, 57

Pantry or food center, 111
Paper sack funnel, 155
Peace of mind, benefit of
  streamlining, 5, 10-11
Pet center, garage, 145-146
Phone book hang-up, 114
Piping tip, in sewing, 135
"Place-for-everything-and-
  everything-in-its-place" advice,
  1, 9
Preparing family, 16-17
Projects and Dreams Worksheet, 79,
  80-81

Quality over quantity, 2, 21, 35-36,
  72, 120
Questions, evaluation, 16, 19-21, 35

Reading, suggested, 169
"Reasonable cleaning opportunity"
  for children, 49, 51, 60-61, 63,
  93
Recycling center, garage, 142-143
Resistance from others, 27
Room-by-room approach to
  streamlining, 3
Room-within-a-room furniture
  arrangements, 77, 85
Rooms, purposes of, 44-45

Sandwich center, 112

Savings in time and energy, benefit of
  streamlining, 5-7
Scheduling for streamlining, 29, 30
Seasonal items, 21, 99
Sewing room, 132-136
  equipment, 135
  fabric details, 133
  mending, 135-136
  notions and trims, 133-135
  patterns, 132-133
Shuffle lifestyle, 2
Skeleton of home, healthy, 15, 119,
  126, 158
"Someplace else"
  container, 17
  temporary catchall, 18
  things, 18
Space(s), 12-13, 24
  more, benefit of streamlining, 4,
    7-8
Spaghetti bag, 96
Sports equipment center, garage,
  145
Stenciling, 58, 66, 75, 169
Storage
  at your fingertips, 31, 63, 122
  books, 88
  cabinets, closets, cupboards, 119-
    126
  frequently used items, 122
  hang it, 48, 49, 50, 137, 141, 143,
    146, 150
  in garage, 147
  like items, grouping and storing
    together, 8, 16, 21-22, 47-48, 56,
    120
  no storage, bathroom, 50
  seasonal things, 21, 99, 152, 153
  under the bed, 42
Storage area streamlining, 151-158
  back-up system and holding area,
    155
  basic tips, 31, 155
  dead storage, 151
  grocery store arrangement of
    shelving, 155
  home management, 152, 153-155

inventory system, 31, 155, 156-158
paper sack funnel, 155
seasonal/occasional, 21, 152, 153
Streamlining, 2, 4, 5, 8, 9, 16
    baby's room, 55-59
    back porch or deck, 148-150
    basic laws, 12-15
    basic steps, 16-24
    bathroom, 46-54
    benefits of, 4-11
    cabinets, closets, cupboards, 119-126
    don'ts, 26
    enforcing the changes, 30, 69, 122
    family room, 85-89
    garage, 137-150
    kids' rooms, 60-69
    kitchen, 19, 90-118
    laundry area, 127-131
    living room, 70-84
    master bedroom, 34-45
    motto, 6
    preparation for, 3, 16-19, 27-33
    sewing room, 132-136
    starting, the best place, 2, 34-35
    steps, 15-24
    storage area, 151-158
Stress, less, benefit of streamlining, 11
Suggested reading, 169
Supplies for streamlining, 31-32
Surface mess versus surface neatness, 13-15

Tableware center, 93-94
Three price tags, 13
Time, more, benefit of streamlining, 4, 5-7, 22
Toaster, what to do with, 112
To Do file folder, 115
To File container for streamlining, 17, 71
Tool and building supply center, garage, 139-140
Tossers, 1, 3, 9
Treasure box, 16, 22-24

Under the bed considerations, 42
Utensils, 94, 96, 97, 116, 117, 118

Vanity, bathroom, 47-49

Wallpaper alternatives, 58, 75
Walls
    baby's room, 58
    bathroom vanity, 48
    inside closet, 36-37
    kids' rooms, 66-67
    kitchen, 91, 118
    living room, 72-74
    master bedroom, 43
Wants and Needs List, 31-32, 33, 61
Work centers chart, kitchen, 91, 104-105

Yard and garden center, garage, 140-141

More Great Books to Help You Get The Most Out Of Life!

Deniece Schofield's Kitchen Organization Tips and Secrets—Make work in your kitchen more organized and productive—from storage to cleaning to grocery shopping and more! You'll discover time-saving strategies to integrate kitchen work into your hectic schedule and suggestions for making the most of the space you have. *#70326/$12.99/240 pages/50 b&w illus./paperback*

Stephanie Culp's 12-Month Organizer and Project Planner—This is the get-it-done planner! If you have projects you're burning to start or yearning to finish, you'll zoom toward accomplishment by using these forms, "To-Do" lists, checklists and calendars. *#70274/$12.99/192 pages/paperback*

How to Have a 48-Hour Day—Get more done and have more fun as you double what you can do in a day! Aslett reveals reasons to be more productive everywhere—and what "production" actually is. You'll learn how to keep accomplishing despite setbacks, ways to boost effectiveness, the things that help your productivity and much more. *#70339/$12.99/160 pages/120 illus./paperback*

How To Get Organized When You Don't Have the Time—You keep meaning to organize the closet and clean out the garage, but who has the time? Culp combines proven time-management principles with practical ideas to help you clean-up key trouble spots in a hurry. *#01354/$11.99/216 pages/paperback*

Streamlining Your Life—Tired of the fast-track life? Stephanie Culp comes to the rescue with quick, practical, good-humored and helpful solutions to life's biggest problem—not having enough time. You'll get practical solutions to reoccurring problems, plus a 5-point plan to help you take care of tedious tasks. *#10238/$11.99/142 pages/paperback*

You Can Find More Time for Yourself Every Day—Professionals, working mothers, college students—if you're in a hurry, you need this time-saving guide! Quizzes, tests and charts will show you how to make the most of your minutes! *#70258/$12.99/208 pages/paperback*

Don Aslett's Clutter-Free! Finally and Forever—Free yourself of unnecessary stuff that chokes your home and clogs your life! If you feel owned by your belongings, you'll discover incredible excuses people use for allowing clutter, how to beat the "no-time" excuse, how to determine what's junk, how to prevent recluttering and much more! *#70306/$12.99/224 pages/50 illus./paperback*

Slow Down and Get More Done—Determine the right pace for your life by gaining control of worry, making possibilities instead of plans and learning the value of doing "nothing." *#70183/$12.99/192 pages/paperback*

Make Your House Do the Housework, Revised Edition—Take advantage of new work-saving products, materials and approaches to make your house keep itself in order. You'll discover page after page of practical, environmentally-friendly new ideas and methods for minimizing home cleaning and maintenance. This book includes charts that rate materials and equipment. Plus, you'll find suggestions for approaching everything from simple do-it-yourself projects to remodeling jobs of all sizes. *#70293/$14.99/208 pages/215 b&w illus./paperback*

How To Conquer Clutter—Think of this book as a "first aid guide" for when you wake up and find that clutter has once again taken over every inch of available space you have. You'll get insightful hints from A to Z on how to free yourself from clutter's grasp. *#10119/$11.99/184 pages/paperback*

Conquering the Paper Pile-Up—Now there's hope for even the messiest record keeper! You'll discover how to sort, organize, file and store every piece of paper in your office and home. Plus, you'll get instruction on how to deal with life's most important documents! *#10178/$11.95/176 pages/paperback*

Don't Be A Slave to Housework—Discover how to get your house in order and keep it that way. You'll learn to arrange a schedule to get your housework done, get your spouse in on the housekeeping action, unclutter your home, do preventative maintenance, use more brain power than elbow grease to clean and much more! *#70273/$10.99/176 pages/paperback*

Clutter's Last Stand—You think you're organized, but your drawers and closets explode when opened. Get out of clutter denial! Aslett provides humorous anecdotes, cartoons, quizzes and lots of practical advice to help you get rid of clutter in every aspect of your life. *#01122/$11.99/280 pages/paperback*

Office Clutter Cure—Discover how to clear out office clutter—overflowing "in" boxes, messy desks and bulging filing cabinets. Don Aslett offers a cure for every kind of office clutter that hinders productivity—even mental clutter like gossip and office politics. *#70296/$9.99/192 pages/175 illus./paperback*

Is There Life After Housework?—All you need to take the dread out of housework are some ingenious ideas and a little inspiration. You'll find both in Aslett's revolutionary approach designed to free you from the drudgery of housework! *#10292/$10.99/216 pages/250 b&w illus./paperback*

The Organization Map—Defeat clutter and disorganization! This battle plan offers dozens of step-by-step and room-by-room put-to-use worksheets and checklists. *#70224/$12.99/208 pages/paperback*

Confessions of an Organized Homemaker—Discover hundreds of ideas and techniques on how to unclutter your home and take control of your life. Plus, you'll find motivation builders, consumer product information and more! *#70240/$10.99/224 pages/20 b&w illus./paperback*

Confessions of a Happily Organized Family—Deniece Schofield shows you how to work as a family to restore—or establish for the first time—a comfortable sense of order to your home. You'll find specific organizational techniques for making mornings and bedtimes more peaceful, making chores fun, storing kids' stuff and much more! *#01145/$10.99/248 pages/paperback*

Holiday Fun Year-Round with Dian Thomas—A year-round collection of festive crafts and recipes to make virtually every holiday a special and memorable event. You'll find exciting ideas that turn mere holiday observances into opportunities to exercise imagination and turn the festivity all the way up—from creative Christmas gift-giving to a super Super Bowl party. *#70300/$19.99/144 pages/paperback*

The Consumer's Guide to Understanding and Using the Law—Practical advice—not legal mumbo-jumbo—will teach you your rights in family law, real estate, criminal law and more! *#70236/$14.99/288 pages/paperback*

Into the Mouths of Babes—Discover 175 economical, easy-to-make, vitamin-packed, preservative-free recipes. Plus, you'll find a shopper's guide to whole foods, methods to cope with allergies, a comprehensive prenatal and infant nutrition resource and what not to put into the mouths of babes! *#70276/$9.99/176 pages/paperback*

Gary Branson's Home Repairs and Improvements on a Budget—Save money with step-by-step instructions that show you how to quiet floor noises, prevent drain clogs, locate wall studs and hundreds of other easy do-it-yourself projects! *#70247/$16.99/160 pages/128 b&w illus./paperback*

Let the
"CLUTTER THERAPISTS"©
Get the *Rats* Out of Your *Race* !©

Alice and Pauline, both specialists in the field of Home Management and Child Development, were invited as the "Clutter Therapists" to the *Good Morning America* show to treat one of their most famous patients, Erma Bombeck. The authors are active consultants and speakers who would like to share with you their humorous, information-packed seminar series, "Get the Rats Out of Your Race!©"

For more information on "Get the Rats Out of Your Race!©":

PAULINE HATCH	**ALICE FULTON**
105 East 36th Place	4508 South Kent
Kennewick, WA 99337	Kennewick, WA 99337
509/582-2459	509/586-0269